T'ai Chi Ch'uan

THE
Internal
Tradition

Ron Sieh

North Atlantic Books
Berkeley, California

Published by
North Atlantic Books
P.O. Box 12327
Berkeley, California 94701

Cover and book design by Paula Morrison
Printed in the United States of America

T'ai Chi Ch'uan: The Internal Tradition is sponsored by the
Society for the Study of Native Arts and Sciences, a nonprofit educational corporation whose goals are to develop an educational
and crosscultural perspective linking various scientific, social, and
artistic fields; to nurture a holistic view of arts, sciences, humanities,
and healing; and to publish and distribute literature on the relationship of mind, body, and nature.

Contents

Thank you,

    Peter Ralston for his teachings; Gloria Starr for her patience in turning me computer-literate; and the crew at North Atlantic Books, especially Richard Grossinger without whom this book would not have happened.

Preface

I met Ron when he came to my school in the late 70's. During our first conversation he mentioned Tae Kwon Do. At some point I let slip an opinion (as I am prone to do) that most martial artists really don't know how to kick. This to a Tae Kwon Do stylist, of course, demanded some sort of challenge, which Ron supplied. I accepted. I told Ron to kick me, and as he began to comply, I moved. He continued attempting to follow my request, and I continued my maneuvers. After some time I stopped and pointed out that he had not only not kicked me, he hadn't even thrown a kick. Ron, being an intelligent person, realized that he couldn't have successfully completed any of his kicks, so he didn't try. At this juncture, many martial artists, egos having been hurt, have merely gone away, indignant and upset. Ron stayed. At the time he didn't understand what had taken place, but he was open and sensitive enough to realize that something had occurred that was beyond his present level of experience. And so Ron and I began a relationship.

Ron is quick to grasp things. Over the years he applied himself and worked very hard to master what Cheng Hsin is about. Cheng Hsin is the name I have given to the endeavor of understanding and directly experiencing the dynamics, principles, and very nature of any matter—particularly the matter of "Being." He has his own particular interests, but the essence and spirit of the work, which is by far the most important part, he embraced wholeheartedly. It is a spirit of questioning, honesty, not-knowing, self-inspection, and grounded as well as open investigation. Ron is committed to empowering others in this teaching. I am very pleased that this work is being continued in so many forms. I support Ron in his work because it is also mine. It is essential that people are supported in waking up and taking on these studies in an authentic and responsible manner; to go beyond belief and opinion, concept and hearsay, to a genuine and direct experience—to take it on as their own. In this book he pursues this course.

I think it is time that T'ai Chi enthusiasts of all schools begin to take stock of what the art is really about. Until recently T'ai Chi has mainly been practiced in Asia, and so for the last twenty or thirty years it seemed as if all that Western students could do was to learn and believe. Now, however, enough genuine teaching has passed cultural boundaries that it is our responsibility to access and experience for ourselves the truth or lack of truth in anything handed down. I think it is time to move the whole field and study of T'ai Chi on to something even more real, powerful, and honest than what we have been doing up to now. I truly acknowledge and support Ron in this effort.

No principle or dynamic is the exclusive territory of anyone or any system or any art. What we discover we must discover for ourselves, even though this is usually done with the help of others. Those who know me well know that my favorite quote is this one: "A warrior is measured according to this: That he learns from the dregs of the ancients and extracts clear liquid from them." (Chozan Shissai, 18th century Swordmaster.) Ron has truly made this his task. Bravo! And like all good teachers he continues to push on. Well done!

It is said that "imitation is the sincerest form of flattery." In reading Ron's book I was pleased to see so much of what I am committed to myself, reflected and clearly expressed in his words. Since many people know that I hold flattery as a self-serving manipulation, let me say instead that I feel very acknowledged.

Peter Ralston

Introduction

When I was a young Cub Scout I first expressed interest in becoming a martial artist because I was scared and wanted to learn how to fight. I remember lying and telling my peers in Cub Scouts that I was taking Karate lessons. Only a quick phone call home saved me from a fight I surely would have lost. Those years I felt small, weak, and ugly. The course of my life was something I had not even considered controlling.

Then one day in eighth-grade biology I realized I had some power. A guy I wasn't used to being pushed around by hit me. I defended myself. After surrendering for so long, I defended myself. I swung the kid into a wall. He was hurt. Much more than experiencing concern about his pain, I was exhilarated. I was the cause. A part of me died then. After that I became much more concerned with who I hung out with—that is, were they were cool or could they fight?

Growing up in an environment that scared the hell out of me and having spent very little of my time actually in my body participating in that environment, I suddenly experienced the smallest realization of having power as opposed to simply being at the mercy of any given situation. I realized that I no longer had to censor what I wanted to say to people out of fear of being humiliated or hit. That was in Junior High.

In Senior High I was still small and skinny, but I had learned how to strut and act as if I knew what I was doing. A fight in tenth grade set the tone for my next two years. There was a rather firm hierarchy at Lincoln High in Bloomington, Minnesota. Number One of course was Mike or maybe Tim (they had never tangled so it was an unknown), but we all knew whom they had fought or intimidated, so it was agreed it would have been a glorious match.

Mainly ours was a hierarchy of intimidation rather than the hard evidence of fights. Knowing how to strut and act tough was the key to success. I fought "number four" in the ranking. He was the best friend of number one (in reality he was probably much lower than fourth), and I guess I won. Neither of us got hurt, but I did cut his mouth; and there was blood. Then his good friend stopped the fight. I was in heaven—the crowds in the halls would part for me; people thought I was cool. I was still just as scared, but I had acquired a facade.

While in the Army in 1971 learning how to put together Pershing missiles, I took my first class in Karate. Although I didn't like the teacher, it was a true formal class in the martial arts. I remember other Black Belts showing up who I thought had higher skill than the teacher. The teacher would become very aggressive and try to hurt them. I should have realized then that aggression and jealousy were not a fluke on the pure landscape of martial arts. The class broke up after about six months. I also did some boxing in the Army with a guy from Louisiana who had fought in the Golden Gloves.

I started Tae Kwon Do in 1974. It was about that time the movie *Billy Jack* came out. For some Bruce Lee was a

2

hero; for me it was Billy Jack—someone noble, unassuming, deep, able to kick ass. He defended his people; his cause was just.

Moon Kim was my instructor. He was my ideal of a master: incredibly skilled, funny, inspiring, happy, he inspired respect. Remember Billy Jack in his first movie: "I'm going to kick you on the left side of your face with my left foot and there's nothing you can do about it." Wonderful, eh? The second movie, the spinning kick. WOW! The spinning kick was so cool! I got it down. Moon Kim had an awe-inspiring spinning kick. Any kick he did was a work of art.

I was good at Tae Kwon Do, had long hair, was left of center, and willing to defend my friends and our "way of life" to the death. I was also very angry and afraid of losing. Fear remained the motivation behind my involvement in the martial arts. My guess now is that most martial artists start for the same reason. Power is very attractive to a young man. I was angry that I was picked on growing up and scared it would happen again.

I think—and most martial artists think—that someday we will be called upon to use our art. Most martial artists haven't been and they are curious. Only in defense of others can the fighter's narcissism be transcended. Right? Perhaps later after the fight, when appreciation is showered upon us, narcissistic pride rears its head again. Well, that is how my fantasy goes.

In 1976 I experienced a catalyzing event. I was on a bicycle trip with a friend in southeast Minnesota—pretty country in the bluffs overlooking the Mississippi—when a carload of (I called them "rednecks" at the time) drove by and threw a beer can at me. (Did they yell "Hippie!" too? I did have a ponytail.) I gave them the finger. They circled back to harass me. Little did they know I was a Karate hot shot with heroic ideas. Well, I was humiliated—me with the technical skill

3

to beat up dozens and so proud of my spinning kick, too. I had never really faced anyone who was out to hurt me.

Training at the school was a laboratory. We pulled our punches; it's called point Karate. Well, I gave the first (and only) guy out the door a beautiful round kick to the solar plexus. Of course I pulled it; that is what I was trained to do. My opponent got pissed off. Then I learned the hard way that a repertoire of fancy techniques is meaningless if there is no one in that well-trained body. I had checked out, went away, spaced out.

Moon Kim had not taught me how to fight; he taught me Tae Kwon Do, and when the shit hit the fan, I got slammed. It was the first time someone wanted to kick my ass (no laboratory), his intention was bigger than mine, and it manifested with me on the ground, physically unhurt except for some scratches (I had it together that much) but shaken, humiliated. I was a bad Tae Kwon Do dude and I was crushed. A reality check.

I had never studied fear; I had lived it, covered it up, but never studied it. I was used to people not messing with me because they knew I studied Tae Kwon Do. Well, after that incident I became disillusioned with my approach, what I now call the "external" approach.

I moved to California either to learn Aikido or T'ai Chi Ch'uan or to become a Rolfer. After studying with a couple of T'ai Chi teachers and becoming dissatisfied rather quickly (after all, I wanted to become a better fighter and most T'ai Chi instructors only teach a set of movements), I was introduced to Peter Ralston. Then my real training began.

Learning martial arts and becoming very good at them was very important to me. I went to class four nights a week and Saturday mornings and practiced all the time. I mean "all the time." I became deeply involved in the teachings and I was committed to realizing them moment by moment and knowing when I wasn't. I was committed to a relaxation so deep boundaries would disappear and the practice would become effortless. Paradox. It takes intent maintained and sustained to be attentive; that is the practice. In the matchup you watch how your partner perceives the relationship, how he (or she) sees what you do and how they don't see. Being open enough to see that, yet holding the intention of not getting hit, or yielding to a push and hitting or finding your partner's center, maybe even uprooting him—all imply paradox. Leading someone is giving him a target and making sure that he sees it. Then we can move the target (we, us) so as to create a disadvantage for the opponent. When his mind wanders from the target and he turns (boredom) to a preferred target, we see it and grab his attention with yet a new target. The opponent is continually double-weighted. All this is done in a relaxed and effortless manner yet always with deep commitment and intention. This is what Peter taught.

I have studied with other teachers since my time with Peter, including his teachers. I have studied other martial arts since then too, but I have not had a teacher who has left such a profound impression. Through Peter I was introduced to "internal" martial arts.

The study of martial arts can increase our capacity to "hold" sensation. In a small gathering, Aikidoist Richard Strozzi Heckler told us he thought a source of violence is people's inability to handle their own pain; they can't handle it so they project it onto others. They cause pain. I think that is true. People feel, then go into reaction, a knee-jerk lashing-out of "self-protection."

We have all met (maybe even loved) people who constantly need reassurance and, when met with anything not to their liking, lash out. Having an enemy gives us credentials—even more than credentials, a reference point. I know I exist because someone else is fighting me. Narrowly defined boundaries establish their existence; space is terrifying.

We have the opportunity to be more than who we think we are and live in a world much greater and more diverse than we can imagine.

The skill of being able to tell how we arrive at our perception is invaluable and is the number-one priority for living in the body.

How do we know that we exist? Deep physical experience connects us with the world, a world that is new and fresh, always accessible, providing us with moment-by-moment, accurate information about whatever we are in contact with.

Feeling the body deeply is a necessary prerequisite for any skill that demands having a body, or for that matter, simply being. It is the foundation of our experience as bodies. Without sensation we have no body, our experience is restricted to symbols rather than the substance of the world. To the degree we feel our bodies we are grounded in phenomenal reality. I think, therefore I am, is a scary thought.

I am not anti-concept or anti-symbol; they work and are useful. I can look at a bus schedule (a concept), go to the bus stop (a concept), and catch a bus (also a concept) and go to a movie. It works; it's a gift.

In the martial arts, or any discipline that demands accurate information for its performance, to confuse a symbol or thought with reality (say an incoming punch) can have devastating results. Yet in the majority of martial arts that have moved away from actual combat, we fail to study and make a discipline out of noticing how we arrive at our information. Even in an event like boxing, amateur or professional, this skill is recognized but neither studied nor practiced. You either have it or you don't.

Many people learn the T'ai Chi set of movements to improve their health, to get in touch with their bodies and relax. Good stuff, very important stuff, but we can go deeper.

For many involved in the martial arts, training is a way of hardening against an enemy, of changing a situation in a self-directed manner. When I did Tae Kwon Do I had much more of a block/punch attitude towards the world. Listening was not a significant part of the teaching. Though I have seen clear examples of my teacher's listening, his teachings did not communicate it. On the other hand, the Vipassana retreats I have experienced have been very supportive of the listening way of being. Mindfulness is the foundation of Vipassana. Mindful martial arts are a rare find and a worthy study.

A powerful martial artist is one who surrenders to his or her opponent and molds himself to their actions.

One hears much about animals in the Chinese martial arts. Some styles are named after and mimic certain animals: White Crane, Praying Mantis, White Tiger, Eagle Claw, etc. This suggests that the techniques of the arts were created from the observations of how particular animals move and fight.

Animals have much to teach us concerning true commitment and doubtlessness of action. They are not torn between conflicting loyalties nor are they often stunned by their own fear. A raccoon is a terrible adversary when cornered or otherwise threatened. I feared for my eighty-pound dog's life when, against my wishes, he forced a fight upon a raccoon half his weight. The sheer ferocity expressed in the sounds and energy of a cornered animal is staggering. The animal is not concerned with technique, nor is there any loss of bodily integrity because of mindlessness. There is no separation between aspects of itself, its mind, its body, its spirit, etc. Animal spirit is a worthy study.

The mimicking of an actual animal movement (as if its power resides in mechanical technique) is an interesting but limiting endeavor. Animals fight as their nature dictates. A tiger does not fight like a praying mantis. As humans we can mimic the actions of either. We are very adaptable, more so than any other animal on the planet. To restrict ourselves to the movements of a particular style is foolish. Our intelligence and resilience are better suited to something else, something that is amenable to our nature, our stature.

This theme of deep connection and realization is something that will be surfacing again and again within the context of this book. Challenging assumptions about the martial arts, about ourselves, and relationships in general allows for a deeper experience to arise. Stay loose in the challenging part, too; it is easy to slide into exclusivity and apathy.

Most martial artists I have met are confined to what they know about individual martial arts, and not enough investigation has gone into what I consider to be the foundation of all martial arts, which is simply being awake and open to things as they are. It is less in our interest to see the world as collection of adversaries (other schools, other people, other dogmas, etc.) than to use our ability and willingness to cultivate allies and bring people together—not bringing them together so they will be on our side and put us in a more powerful position to fight our enemies, but out of simple compassion and kindness. The most decisive manner of winning a battle is not to fight with, but to blend with our partner. After many years of being a martial artist, I have found that true victory is attained out of cultivated friendship rather than imposing one's will on defeated enemies.

Introduction to T'ai Chi Ch'uan

T'ai Chi is often translated as primordial, undifferenti-
ated and absolute. It is prior to duality. Ch'uan is fist;
yet T'ai Chi Ch'uan as an art is essentially formless. If
you have been involved in the study of the art you've probably heard the mythology before. This time consider it as
possibly true and reflect on the appearance of the form that
you do. "Ch'uan" connotes manifestation; we are human
bodies, we can't (or I can't) turn into something else. The
formless is given form through the body, while the body
remains loose. It's your form. It's not someone else's. It's your
art, so what you do is you.

T'ai Chi is an art whereby (once realized) we live our sense
of immersion in life. This is done deliberately, with commitment, not in some wishy-washy sort of way. We relax
and surrender to the fundamental ground of reality rather
than flit around in search of something.

T'ai Chi Ch'uan is a martial art that is well suited to life.
There is no blocking, no fighting another's strength. The
power is effortless; mindfulness is its fundamental practice. Of
course there is a gap between theory and practice among
many T'ai Chi practitioners. All know the ideal and stum-
ble towards it. Seeing (if we do) our resistance to such sur-

render is a step towards surrender. The Karate I have done supports a more block/punch, faster/harder attitude toward conflict, although I have seen what I would call a more internal expression of Karate.

There seems to be a paradox here: how do you know you are practicing T'ai Chi Ch'uan? Well, it is easy; it says so on the outside of your school; it says what you are learning. You know who your teacher is and who your fellow students are, right? The principles of T'ai Chi, the relaxing, sinking, unifying, etc., have to be "known" in order for them to be studied and communicated. Yet "knowing" them can also be a barrier to a deeper experience of them.

The classics are the literary foundation of T'ai Chi Ch'uan and well-regarded. But after having read the classics and intellectually understanding them, I wonder does that knowledge really—I mean *really*—make us any better at T'ai Chi Ch'uan? It could be that we are just better at understanding the classics.

I stopped by Shambhala Books today. There were many books on T'ai Chi Ch'uan, its philosophy, history, stuff on the *I Ching* and how the trigrams hook up with the moves of the set, more stuff about how each move strengthens this, that meridian, interpretations of the classics, yin/yang stuff. It is all a fun intellectual exercise, but what a bunch of crap! T'ai Chi Ch'uan is dead.

We give it life. If we do not discover what the founders of the art discovered, it is all dead.

What the hell does power from the ground directed through the waist *mean?* Sounds great! We all know the T'ai Chi rap, right? Relaxed, sunk, unified, blah, blah!!!!! The T'ai Chi classics are the literary parameter by which to gauge one's direction, but simply reading them does not necessarily enhance one's ability to manifest their principles.

The principles that allow for powerful and appropriate interaction are not the property of any teacher or particular lineage, but are the inheritance of the human race.

I have had several friends who studied in the Cheng Man-Ch'ing tradition of T'ai Chi Ch'uan. These people have as the foundation and trademark of their art the T'ai Chi set that was modified and shortened by Cheng Man-Ch'ing. They are very meticulous concerning the choreography of that set: fingertips level with the eye, just so far away from the body, the weight exactly seventy percent on one foot, thirty percent on the other. Typically there is no deviation. There is also a pride and certain arrogance in having studied with the man who many consider the authority, the lineage holder (although the Yang family disagrees) of Yang Cheng Fu's style of T'ai Chi Ch'uan. Yet none of the disciples come close to what Cheng Man-Ch'ing could do, and all seem unwilling to explore outside the dogma of their teacher's teaching.

When I studied with Gin Foon Mark and learned his Chi Kung, I heard for the first time the notion of "hands": "try someone's hands," "learn their hands." "Hands" is someone's feel, the essential core of their personal art.

In descriptions, T'ai Chi Ch'uan is often referred to as a Chinese art. It did originate there and I am sure more Chinese study it than people of any other nationality. My central teacher in T'ai Chi was not Chinese, and for me it is not a Chinese art. Peter Ralston did not teach a Chinese art; he taught his hands. For many years I did "Peter's hands" as well as I could. Now I do MY hands.

To attain real skill we need to take responsibility for our art. We take ownership, or we will be doing someone else's art, Ueshiba's art, Funikoshi's art, whomever's art. I have heard that one of Bruce Lee's fears was that Jeet Kune Do would calcify into a system.

It is necessary to be responsible for our own evolution, to not give our power of choice and free inquiry over to dogmas, teachers, or gurus. It is important to have teachers, but it is important to move beyond what we have been taught.

When I explore the effects of gravity on my body, it is not my teacher's gravity that allows for pressure against the earth. His personal gravity is charisma. Clearly it is not to our advantage to substitute another person's words for our own experience, though it is advantageous to seek the counsel of those who have gone where we have not. This is the dilemma every serious student eventually faces.

This unwillingness to explore and discover means the death of not only Yang T'ai Chi Ch'uan but any art that is held to a narrow interpretation by its artists. Sure, there is a great rap involved, and it is the responsibility of the student to learn it, but it is not necessarily open to real inquiry: "Sink" means this, not that; "relax" means this, not that; etc.

Typically T'ai Chi is not a growing, vital art but a study of shapes and the memorization of a philosophy. If a student has a problem with something, say the ability to put the position of the waist at a certain angle, the teacher sets the student in the "proper" stance rather than adjusting his or her stance to allow for any peculiarity in body structure. Students try to force their body in a shape that mechanically severs them from the ground. Many students sacrifice common sense to adhere to some particular dogma. I recently met someone who was told by his T'ai Chi instructor to stand with one's weight in the heels of the feet. Most T'ai Chi practitioners have heard (Yang school) the knee should not go past the toe, that this keeps the weight of the body from being exclusively in the ball of the foot; it keeps one from overextending and throwing oneself off balance. Anyway, this guy was walking around on his heels; his set was a constant battle to keep his weight in his heels and not fall over backwards. He sacrificed his common sense for "something greater."

It is often very hard for beginning students to know what is best. A teacher able to "walk his talk" is a good sign, particularly in T'ai Chi where there is no recognized notion of what "good and bad" T'ai Chi is. There are many who do not, cannot, do what they teach others to do. They often respond to criticism by stating that they too are just students on the path. If after three years of study they do not have a handle on relaxation and effortless power, they are pointed in the wrong direction, whatever they are teaching.

It is possible to acquire a taste for more fundamental goals. One can have the goal of being grounded, or moving powerfully from one foot to another, or achieving relaxed power and then exploring its extension. One can explore what feels grounded or powerful. Rather than taking a shape even if it does not feel right, change the shape so it feels more powerful. Do not adopt the idea that if one does a powerless but correctly mimicked shape for ten years one will become powerful. The founders of the art were powerful people, and I do not think it was because they practiced certain shapes. They explored realms of power and were willing to let go of dogma. I do not mean to imply that maps are not important, but often one does mistake the map for the territory. Teachers are important; teachers can be a barrier.

William Chen, the T'ai Chi master noted for his skill and willingness to explore and change, said that T'ai Chi scholars typically are not good at T'ai Chi Ch'uan. Chen's knee goes beyond his toe; his knees seem to buckle inside the direction of his toes; he breaks a lot of *rules*. He is incredibly skilled and functional at this art. He also studied many years with Cheng Man-Ch'ing.

(After you have understood the classics and gained the ability to manifest their teachings physically, energetically, and mindfully, would that mean the next time you did the set, or pushed hands, you would manifest the teachings? Read that again.)

Most people engaged in T'ai Chi Ch'uan are in denial. They are people who have been doing (not studying) for many years, people who have the rap down and sound very knowledgeable, who swear they are relaxed and yet, when even slightly pressed, quickly resort to bullying. Bullying is different from listening and surrendering; bullying can be taken advantage of. That is, it can if winning is the objective. I have found that people who have not studied T'ai Chi Ch'uan, even other martial artists, are more willing to "invest in loss" than the typical T'ai Chi practitioner.

Blindly following the teachings of an instructor will only add to the legions of the disseminators of dogma. Consciously studying what a teacher has to offer can lead to mastery and a strengthening of the lineage. Again, we must discover what our teachers have discovered . . . unless of course we choose a teacher who merely dispenses knowledge and philosophy and has no real skill. (Although even then, if we study with sincerity what is said, we may discover the experience that initially wrought the words.) It is always the good teacher's wish that their students surpass them.

I am not suggesting that we have no teachers or no respect for past discoveries, but I am asking us to realize for ourselves what mastery is, to realize what the masters realized, not just to believe that relaxation is better than tension, but to soberly investigate the truth of the matter and to question what is relaxation, what is tension. Feel them in your life and move beyond your concepts of relaxation and tension; of "I" and other; of what works and what doesn't. The future of T'ai Chi Ch'uan demands that we realize what the founders realized.

For beginners in the martial arts, our energy is often put into learning moves—memorizing the names of the techniques and in what order they occur. The mindfulness and deep sense of inquiry and investigation necessary for the discovery of the art are put on the back burner. In internal martial arts the choreography is not the art, yet there is no practice, no art without the choreography. We can substitute the word "technique" for "choreography" here; I do not mean to imply that I am talking just about movement. I have made a distinction between the internal techniques and external techniques of coming into our bodies. External techniques can be obviously seen; they are choreography.

If we are learning the choreography of a set of movements, we have the choice of organizing the structure (shape) of the individual movements around internal principles: relax, align with gravity, drain, etc. We can also just learn the choreography on the chance that it (the choreography) will allow us to discover the principles. The latter is the course most beginners unconsciously choose simply because the learning of the movements is demanding enough in itself. Later, when one is accustomed to the movements, principles can be more deeply explored and appreciated. If the principles are not eventually given priority over the shapes taken—that is, if the practitioner thinks that assuming a certain form will allow the discovery of the internal art—the practitioner will end up with a perfect set of moves yet not have a feel for the depth out of which the moves were discovered.

Without form, choreography, technique, it is nearly impossible to learn anything. To make coffee we boil water, grind beans, use equipment properly—filter cone, pot, etc. We have to put the ground beans in the filter, which rests in the cone on the pot that catches the newly made coffee. We pour the hot water over the ground beans. A lot of technique and rules need to be obeyed if our objective is hot coffee.

Through the study of technique, we can refine; for example, we can get better at how much coffee to grind, how much water to use, and then we can adjust each time according to the result. It is the adjusting that makes the art.

We learn punches, kicks, pushes—many techniques. In more internal schools these are studied and refined so they may be done in a more relaxed and effortless manner while still being powerful and grounded.

A new student quickly finds there are a lot of T'ai Chi sets or forms out there, many different ways the art can look; yet the basic principles are the same (relax, sink, align with gravity, use the whole body). When doing sets or two-person work you want to move precisely what you feel. You want to feel your body (at least), so you move what you feel rather than the bulk or the meat. The latter requires effort. To move your body, feel your body and move what you feel. Feel the space you occupy and, if there are pieces missing, fill it out.

Typically the martial arts are characterized by how they arrive at power: the external, by muscular effort; the internal, relaxed and effortlessly. All "karates" are considered external and most of the Cninese arts, plus Judo, Capoeira, and Kali, are lumped into the external category. T'ai Chi Ch'uan, Hsing I Ch'uan, and Pa Kua are the Chinese internal arts and of course, Aikido is a Japanese art. All others are external. This is generally the belief of those who study T'ai Chi, Pa Kua, Hsing I, or Aikido. There is a flow in the internal arts that is missing from the external ones. In the external there is a quality of fighting, of pushing against the way things are, to change what is happening to better fit our "plan." In the internal tradition a more inclusive approach is cultivated, a quality of non-interference, of using your opponents' strengths to your advantage without the struggle to change them.

If it is attractive to you, I would recommend a variety of martial arts. Study with many teachers, be open to everything, and trust yourself, your deep self. Before taking off to study another art (unless the one you are taking isn't "it"), learn at least one of these arts rather well. Learning a little bit of many arts has its advantages, especially when what you learn is some of the best of each particular art. But if you keep changing arts before, say, you can do a side kick (if you're studying Karate)—or one of the kicks or punches peculiar to any particular art—you will never be good at any technique. Skill in executing technique is very important. It is the Ch'uan of T'ai Chi. Yet an art which is limited to the study of technique is not an internal martial art.

External T'ai Chi is T'ai Chi that puts its focus on form. This is the case whether the form is specific shapes taken with the body or visualization which has nothing to do with what is presently happening. It is T'ai Chi which is not relaxed, not unified; it is T'ai Chi which is focused instead of inclusive.

In internal T'ai Chi Ch'uan we acknowledge our present state, physically, emotionally, energetically, and go from there. We want to experience directly what is true and real. This is not done by visualization, mastering forms, hearing stories of great masters, or holding ideas of accomplishment after years of practice, but only by acknowledging what actually is the case in our present situation. Only from such realization do we have the ability to consciously change, transform. This does not mean working anything out, only realization and taking responsibility for ourselves. For example, if I hold my shoulders up and rigid, before I can relax them I must directly, experientially realize them as up and rigid. The next thing is to realize *who* is holding them that way. Who is responsible? Then and only then can I relax them.

I have been studying T'ai Chi and Hsing I since 1976 and I have dabbled in Pa Kua and Aikido. I have studied several of the "karates." All in all, I have done the typical "martial arts bum" routine. I have realized that any art can be internal or external. My Tae Kwon Do teacher was an internal martial artist, though he taught an external art. Aikido, like T'ai Chi, has an internal "rap"; yet most of what I have seen is choreography-oriented and "hard." I have seen what I would consider good Aikido and good T'ai Chi. My point is that the people make martial arts; it is what the teachers and students are up to that define their arts, not the names of the particular styles.

Both internal and external martial arts have power and speed as priorities. The priorities are the same for all martial arts; it is how these are practiced, the way they are attained, that differentiate internal from external.

Many martial artists agree that relaxation is good. The degree to which this is done varies from tense muscular contraction to deep, profound relaxation. My Tae Kwon Do instructor was relaxed; my T'ai Chi Ch'uan instructor was profoundly relaxed. It isn't the art but the person doing the art who is or isn't relaxed.

The push-hands game in T'ai Chi is supposed to be done very relaxed. Most people who do it are not relaxed. I have seen relaxed Wing Chun and "hard" Wing Chun. Relaxed power is internal. Contracted force is external.

I would say most good fighters to a degree are internal martial artists. When we are soft and open to what is happening, responding to our "opponent" rather than strategizing, when we are manifesting relaxed power, we are doing an internal art. It could be Karate, Aikido, or Hsing I Ch'uan; or not.

To move your body, feel your body; move the feeling. Feel the space you occupy; fill the space you occupy with feeling (sensation). It can be much larger than what you see in the mirror. Feel the space around, over, and under you.

18

Sensation is not confined to this (inside) side of your skin. We may ask how one's movement can be well executed and look good without a grasp of the internal principles; yet this is the disguise of most T'ai Chi. Some sets of martial movements demand a grasp of the internal to be performed at all by virtue of the sheer skill needed to do the set. Others, like most T'ai Chi sets, can be choreographically well-performed with tension.

It is important to do this work eventually with a partner so that we have a means of feedback. When in relationship, adjusting and molding oneself toward the goal of blending with our partner's actions is the art. How do we know if what we do has power unless we actually move another body? How do we know if we are truly relaxed until we are pushed?

When working with another in a "choreographed" manner, we experience an element of freshness, of not-knowing (even though we may "know" the choreography). What will happen next must be held open or the practice will take on an air of fakery, pretentiousness. Only with openness can we truly be with what is happening in this moment, and the next, and the next. We reflect the new demand of each moment instead of seeing our plans for the future being dashed by flawed outcomes. We are confined to form and technique, and yet we want to be fluid, formless. Technique is coincidental. Form (technique) follows function; yet without form there is no function.

Choreography is important; don't get me wrong. In Feldenkrais bodywork, "awareness through movement" technique is used to demand the mindfulness of the participants. Without awareness the instructions (techniques) simply could not be done. In the martial arts, techniques are the foundation of any particular art. Yet if the teachings don't delve any deeper than making a technique look good, I get bored. I have found for beginning students that learning a set of moves is their priority; it was mine, along with the skill trained for the execution of the moves. This gives something to train: a ritual that says, "I am a martial artist; I am training and getting better. My 'set' says so."

Martial-arts training starts out to promote physical conditioning, coordination, balance, increased flexibility, and stamina. Sets of moves are taught that support these qualities of training, something a lot of T'ai Chi practitioners do not go through. Being better able to balance on one foot, for example, might be achieved (or not) through the study of T'ai Chi Ch'uan, and yet already having the ability to do so upon beginning training will promote a deeper appreciation of T'ai Chi training. Later we start making subtle distinctions of how we stand on a foot (or both feet, for that matter); then we want to cultivate a feeling of draining into the lower body and the feet.

External to internal can be a natural "occurrence" as we deepen in skill, whatever the art.

There is a school of thought that strongly and rightfully intends that through the study of technique and choreography, the student will discover in each technique what works and what doesn't work. A very gifted student does that. Moving from that discovery to discovering what makes techniques—any technique—work or not is to me, profound.

Ch'i and Internal Martial Arts

The use of Ch'i as a source of individual power has been a much-studied and often elusive part of the martial arts for thousands of years. To experience oneself as not separate from but included in the lifeforce, and in fact guided by it, is attractive (to say the least). To attain such a state is much like arriving home, returning to innocence.

In the internal martial arts, one way in which we use Ch'i is to manifest internal power of Chin (pronounced "gin"). Chin is also called intrinsic strength; it is the compression of Ch'i in the body's tissues then made manifest—for example, in a step, or a punch or push.

Body awareness is the foundation of our art. The practice of awareness is simple in theory yet in actual practice demands the utmost study and attention. It is a very radical practice. One is aware or one is not. Awareness demands living and participating in the moment. This isn't a process. There is no "working through" of anything. For example, whether or not you feel your back depends upon you being aware of your back. Awareness and feeling go together; there is no separation. To be aware is to feel; it is basically a matter of choice. This is where most people get stuck when working with energy. Rather than feel our backs, we want to do something, some technique that will get us in touch with our backs. It is mistaking the map for the territory. Awareness is very simple; it is nothing more than noticing moment by moment what *is*. I want to stress that "nothing more" is the prominent phrase. Don't become infatuated with techniques or exercises, even if they are martial techniques. The technique isn't "it." From one's being mindful and aware of one's body, Ch'i arises as something tangible and therefore workable. So, before Ch'i can be experienced, we must participate and live in our bodies. Put another way: before we can experience, we must feel!

For most people there is a "split," a "gap," separating the lower body from the upper. Actually there can be many splits and gaps including ones separating right from left, particularly the head from the body. Such splits can be seen as metaphors. Head from body = thoughts/feeling; right from left = male/female; upper body from lower body = spirituality/materiality. Feeling the neck can help put the head back on the body. Feeling the abdomen and solar plexus can join upper and lower body. Using both sides of the body equally can join right and left.

The practice of Chi Kung can fill and empower the abdomen and solar plexus. Many men feel very tender and empty in the solar plexus region. In women, the abdomen is the more empty-feeling space. Through breathing in these places either can begin to enliven and fill, actually feeling powerful. This practice can also bring together the body and allow the pressure in the feet to manifest in the upper body, for example, in the hand.

Whatever you experience is energy, because everything *is* energy. Trees, clouds, people, your car; all consist of energy. Increasing our capacity for experience (I am speaking in present tense, present experience) increases our capacity to perceive, to hold and work with energy. There is no separation between you and energy—you are it; this is it. Confusion arises when we put our attention on something other than the present energetic reality. When we have a thought of ourselves separate from the world, we perceive that way. It is usually easy to confuse our thoughts with what is true; yet to realize what is true (which is also to realize energy) simply takes participation. It starts with the body, as it is, no beliefs or opinions, nothing which is not presently there. Feel your skin, all over, completely, then proceed to fill it up, feeling muscles, fat, viscera, blood, bones . . . everything. This is our foundation; we radiate from here.

* * * * *

In the internal martial arts, the cultivation of Ch'i for health has been well documented, yet it is also cultivated for power.

The experience and use of Ch'i as both a source of power and well-being has been the foundation as well as the pinnacle of the martial arts and many other disciplines. Recently there has been an enormous budding of "newer" studies which address the constructive use of energy. Bioenergetics, Rolfing, Reichian work, Alexander technique, Orthobionomy, Trager, Lomi work, Feldenkrais—the list is rather long and the techniques varied, yet through all is a common thread. That is the intention to open restrictions and blocks in the body, to free the energy in the body so it can do its job, which is to be vibrantly alive, spontaneous, and happy.

I am going to go through the principles that I teach to allow the use of Ch'i. They seem very simple and they are not my principles. I, like my teachers, did not create them. As one teacher said, "I merely looked, and they were there."

The first is to relax. Throw open your joints; let your pelvis drop; soften your tissues. This is not that easy an accomplishment; it demands (as usual) paying attention to your body. Before you can relax you have to feel what you want to relax.

Now while you are relaxed and soft and open, align yourself with gravity. One vertebra sits on top of another, like a stack of dishes, relaxed and resting ultimately on the ground. If you are relaxed you are also sunk and grounded. In this state, which is foreign to most people, you can actually start to feel the world around you. You want to put feeling attention into the earth under your feet. You want to cultivate a feeling of actually being plugged into or immersed (at least knee-deep) into the earth.

One actually punches with the solidity and power of the earth. To the one punching it does not feel like power, not as you would expect. One feels relaxed and soft but unified and connected to the ground. The pressure built up in the feet and legs is given direction with the pelvis and manifests as power when contact (fist against body) is made. This is called intrinsic power, for we use the intrinsic rubbery quality of our tissues to manifest power.

From here, being relaxed, sunk, and aligned with gravity, we want to drain or get the feeling of draining from our upper body into our feet and legs. One feels more compressed and dense on the bottom, for this is what we are actually doing. Compressing the tissues in the legs and feet, thus compressing Ch'i in the feet and legs, we relax more, sink more, and compress more Ch'i. The T'ai Chi set is for the cultivation and storing of this compressed Ch'i.

To manifest this compressed Ch'i as power, we use that pressure in our legs and especially on the bottoms of our feet to move or turn our center (located in the area of the navel). It is from here we give direction to the power generated in the feet and legs. So if we want to take a step, we simply lift the foot we want to move and use the pressure built up in the rooted foot to turn the waist, which moves the foot and leg. To continue moving, simply keep doing this: relaxing, sinking, lifting your foot, turning your waist to move the foot, and putting it back down.

During this activity you are feeling and using your body as one piece. That is, you are not moving your limbs without your center directing the movement. To move your limbs otherwise separates your connection to the ground (the source of your power).

Now none of this sounds very mystical and let me assure you it isn't. For those of you who are mystified . . . relax. I studied for years before I could do it. My concern is over-simplification; yet actually it is very simple.

To deliver a punch you simply turn your waist, which moves your arm and fist toward your target. If you hit it in a relaxed and sunken, unified manner, a connection will be made of considerable power.

When fist meets target we remain relaxed, aligned, and bottomed out. We actually displace their weight, their space, with our fist, and with relaxed alignment we put our weight into our fist. We hit, or simply move, with our whole body; everything is involved. They bounce off us.

I don't know what Ch'i is. It is an abstraction. I experience sensation; it is real. We don't feel Ch'i; we feel, period. If we name what we feel, that is an abstraction, an addition. Abstraction is conceptual, raw sensation is non-conceptual, and the two are often confused. But don't believe me; check it out!

Relaxation

We want to be relaxed, so relaxed that if we weren't moving with gravity pushing us into our feet, we would fall down.

We have all had experience in tension and relaxation. Feeling your body *now,* as you read, you will experience both in varying degrees. We have all heard that being relaxed rather than tense is the preference. In my experience, we must feel our bodies in order to realize tension or relaxation. It sounds like common sense, yet most people hold themselves with muscular contraction, and don't feel it.

My dogma is:

- Relaxation is generally more appropriate than tension.

- Using weight and gravity to manifest relaxed effortless power is more powerful than using tense, contracted musculature for power.

- Relaxation is open; openness allows for listening, blending, leading, knowing when and where to move, hit, dodge, etc.

- Tension is closed; it stresses separation from the object of our fear.

- It is our fear and our openness to it that can open us to information regarding the object.

- The feeling of draining and being sunk comes out of relaxation and allows for greater balance and power.

- There is a discipline that encompasses "everything" and cultivates mindfulness.

- With mindfulness we can relax (consciously be relaxed).

Often we do not have a feel for what it is we are to relax. We have to take a step back into ourselves, into the foundation of our experience. If that is conceptual in nature, we simply do not, cannot, relax. Because we do not feel our tension (if there is truly tension), we remain tense all the while thinking about being relaxed. All the while the body stays tense. There is no access. Relaxation is not workable if we don't feel our bodies. Of course if we are in pain, feeling our bodies will be painful. That is the main reason we choose not to feel—because it hurts.

Feeling our bodies with any depth, even at skin level, is not something we are generally trained to do. We learn, "Look both ways before crossing the street" or "Be nice to people" but usually not "Feel your body." Only to the degree we feel do we have the option to relax, to soften. No feeling; no option. Sure, we all have the best reason in the world not to feel. It hurts! Where there is pain we find tension, holding. So, feel the pain and relax.

We often associate (confuse) relaxation with lack of discipline (the sustaining of intent through will) and discipline with a much narrower, tighter (constipated, tense) approach than we need to accomplish our goal . . . as if burning more calories will help to improve our concentration. T'ai Chi is a discipline of the mind. We move our sensation—what we feel ourselves to be—through a series of movements called the T'ai Chi form. What we use to direct our movement is not helped by physical (or mental) contraction, tension. Movement should be effortless; there should be no more effort in doing in a T'ai Chi set than in walking—less in fact, since we are actively engaged in using the ground as the source of power (not that we do not also want to do this when walking).

What it takes to relax starts with a decision. We have to know if "relaxed" is truly what we want to be. In my case, if I were not given a good reason to relax, I would not have. The reason was not that I was chronically tense and on the verge of a heart attack (which by the way would have done the trick, too) but that I had made the decision to get good at T'ai Chi Ch'uan. The only way I saw this ever happening, particularly since I was getting powerful feedback concerning my skill (and lack of it) from my training, was to relax deeply and open to "things as they are." As realized through any potent regimen of bodywork, this has a profound effect on the psyche, since our strongest beliefs of who we are and what is going on are challenged. I would sometimes decide I would rather be, if not tense, then "held."

When standing, we want to be as relaxed as possible and still remain standing. Again, arranging ourselves to accommodate gravity rather than to struggle against it will allow for greater and deeper relaxation. We want to stand into our feet with our bodies stacked upwards from the ground, the piece above resting atop the piece below. This way we don't have to "hold" ourselves up and we can really relax into our feet. Even the legs we want relaxed.

Here it gets kind of tricky—not tricky like a trick but something that demands study. "Relaxed" usually means weak, flaccid, mushy. Well, we obviously can't stand on mush; our legs have to be able to support our weight. In T'ai

Chi the words "full" and "empty" are thrown around a lot. These two words have different meanings at different times. Put simply, the leg that is supporting our weight we call full, the other (since we don't want to be "double weighted") we call empty. Fullness is required to support weight. For example, if we sit on a basketball, particularly a half-full one, it will compress in direct proportion to how much of our weight we give it—that is, up to the point where the ball will support our weight, where the internal pressure will increase but the ball will not visually compress any more. This point at which it supports our weight, I call "bottoming out," or in T'ai Chi lingo, "full." So we want to stand on relaxed, full legs. Notice that the basketball is not working to support the weight, but is at rest. The way to get a feel for this is to minimize the amount of holding we do to stand. Of course without awareness, these are just words. I start by actually tensing my legs, tightening them up, then slowly softening them, doing this several times in a row. Gradually I relax my knees and ankles and actually soften the muscles. As I do so, alignment becomes more important.

There is a difference between relaxed/flaccid/mush and relaxed/full. One is compressed. If we compress mush we will have compression . . . or a mess.

Back to the basketball. It is not the rubber ball itself that is supporting weight but the air inside. The most important function of the ball is to create boundaries in which the air is compressed. No boundaries: no compression. The quality of the ball that allows the compression is its resiliency. If it were wood instead of rubber, rather than allowing for compression it would break. I call a relaxed, soft leg "rubbery." It has an intrinsic elastic quality. A tense, contracted musculature like wood cannot be compressed and, if forced, it will break (rip, strain.)

When we work with relaxing the legs, it is important to

keep in mind that although we want relaxation and compression, we don't want any "leaks." When I stand and am "bottomed out," although my legs are relaxed, they are not mush. My legs will turn weak and mushy if I release the boundaries I have created for compression. I can relax them in a dead sort of way if I release the boundaries. Between tension and this mushy sort of relaxation is "full." It is relaxed and full.

A simple practice I have found helpful is continually minimizing the amount of tension and holding in the legs. Relax the legs, knees, ankles, as much as possible, though still supporting your weight. It is necessary to stand aligned with gravity, pelvis dropped. Knees over the feet point in the same direction as the toes, vertebrae on top of vertebrae like a stack of dishes. Allow gravity to do what it does: push us on the ground. Practice getting a feeling connection between the pressure in your foot and the turning of your pelvis. A simple exercise to do this consists of having your full weight on one leg; with the pressure in that foot turn the pelvis, moving the other leg with it: one piece, one action. Turn the pelvis and step with the other leg.

The earth is basic. Let everything you have—mind and body, thoughts and reactions, plans and avoidance of plans—sink with gravity into your feet to beneath the earth. Relax your intention. Put everything underground where it can support you. Strewn anxiously through your body it can only distract you. Hammer it there with a ritual if you must — make spikes under the earth, photon torpedoes, be creative.

Mindfulness

Mindfulness is the quality of our awareness. Simply being aware. Aware of what? Well, in the martial arts, it is obviously to our advantage to be aware of our bodies, to be aware of the forces in which we live (the prime force being gravity). Only if we are aware of and feeling our bodies will we know if we are relaxed or not, aligned with gravity or not, sunk or not. When we stop feeling our bodies there is essentially no one home to "do" the principles and to notice that we are not "doing" the principles.

After having at least ten instructors in the martial arts, I found only one who ever emphasized mindfulness, and in his regular classes he does not do that much anymore. It seems to be taken for granted, as if the practice of mindfulness is redundant. Yet it is the big secret of the masters and the great wall that must be discovered and embraced. It is hard to do a spinning kick if you don't feel your foot on the ground, and yet people can be frustrated for years before that problem is discovered, if it ever is. I have known people who have practiced T'ai Chi Ch'uan for decades and are not any good at it because they conceptualize rather than feel . . . or they feel and then conceptualize, and freeze the game rather than surrender and create continuity.

One must be committed to the maintenance of mindfulness in the daily routine, not just at the dojo. The more time we are mindful, the more momentum is built up towards being attentive and mindful.

If the only time we consider being in our bodies is two or three hours a week at class time, the momentum just won't be there to bring us into ourselves when we are met with a demand to be mindful. The more time we invest in living in our bodies, the more powerful our interest in doing so becomes. The more time we invest in thinking without our body, the harder it is to stay with feeling.

If we study ourselves, get involved in feeling the body for the two or three hours we go to class and forget it the rest of our life, the odds are against gathering the momentum necessary to cultivate moment-by-moment mindfulness.

Relax, soften
Align with gravity
Drain
Compress
Unify
Sacrum in heel
Pelvis dropped
Breathe in the belly

The martial arts are an excellent arena for the study of mind. In the many games done with others there is opportunity to receive powerful feedback concerning our willingness to be present and to participate.

I have a lot of experience at spacing out and "going away," and I know from such experience that it is not to my advantage to do so, whether I am playing frisbee, giving a massage, or fighting in a full-contact tournament with no protective gear.

Through the study of mindfulness, we learn to make a distinction between our thoughts and what is really happening, or so-called "objective reality." Thinking an apple is not an apple; thinking we are relaxed is not being relaxed. We want to reside in our bodies, not our thoughts of our body but our sensation. We want to hone a distinction between thoughts and sensations.

There is a style of meditation where mindfulness of body sensation (or not mindful) is the central practice. It is called Vipassana or Insight Meditation. Simply, it is having an "anchor" such as the rising and falling of the abdomen or the sensation at the tip of the nose as we breathe where we can let our attention rest. When we notice our mind wandering we simply, without judging, bring our attention back to the anchor. Some people find labeling helpful in this. For example, if we are distracted (or attracted) by sound we simply say to ourselves "hearing" and return to the anchor. If we find ourselves thinking, we say to ourselves "thinking" and return. The practice is noticing and returning.

When we space out or get involved in judging or whatever, rather than analyze or try to figure out why we think so much, we simply come back to the body. The medium through which we cultivate mindfulness is the body. It is a very simple practice that can be incredibly difficult. We go away; we come back. If we get caught on a train of thoughts, the moment we recognize what we are doing we come back to our anchor. Bringing this practice of awareness and mindfulness into our practice of martial arts will add a critical dimension without which we are simply mimicking others and practicing empty technique. From feeling our feet on the ground, we can expand our feeling awareness to include more of our bodies, always returning to our chosen anchor whenever we go away. The practice is returning, continually returning to sensation. Through sensation our experience is immediate, unfettered, and unfiltered by our beliefs and judgments. We are free to reflect our partner's movement and deeply experience the relationship.

This is truly meditation in movement, movement as meditation. Actually we use activity, at every moment, as the object of meditation, staying an active participant in our experience. When we move into what appears to be the mental realm of thinking, we can be with the transition and possibly notice what we give up and what we gain by it.

If our intention is to participate wholly in activity with another person, moving from the feeling realm to the thinking realm has the effect of disconnecting us, as if we actually go elsewhere. We enter a trance, hypnotized by the vision before us. Obviously this is not to our advantage while involved in an activity that demands our attention. Thinking about something else, or even about what is happening before us, disengages us from the activity and we become a spectator. Before or after the action this can be very insightful, but *in* action we space out and fail to dodge the punch or catch the frisbee.

In sitting meditation, there is technique both in the actual sitting—comfortable posture, straight spine, relaxed, etc.—and what we "do" with our attention. The discipline is coming back to our breath after noticing we have left it, over and over again, coming back. Usually after a period of practice we find we don't leave so often. The technique of returning cannot be accomplished without noticing we have left being mindful; yet it is a *technique,* and mindfulness is not confined to its parameters. From where do we return and to what do we return? What leaves; who are we? Is it possible for us to leave? All this can be explored with mindfulness.

We either are involved in the technique of staying with the breath or not. To the observer, in both cases the person is sitting.

(Usually meditation is done sitting on a cushion with legs crossed "Indian style." The cushion should have our hips higher than the knees. The back is comfortably straight, not rigid, but more aligned with gravity so we can relax without holding. Even after five minutes of this we realize how little time we spend in the body.)

It can be difficult to feel the whole body when doing the set—in fact, when doing anything. Choosing an area of the body, say the hands or feet, as an anchor to come back to can be helpful. When doing any activity, feeling your feet on the ground will increase balance and stability, so I often use this as the anchor. Do the set while feeling your feet on the ground and, when you become involved in something else—for example, thinking or spacing out or whatever—simply come back to the feeling of "feet on the ground."

The keynotes remain: simple sensation, feeling our existence, feeling the edge of our skin, feeling the air, feeling myself on the chair and the pen in my hand on the paper, my back against the chair, how my breathing presses against it, inside the body its denseness and warmth.

In fighting, the keynotes are: feeling others and the things around me—my movement, my actions; their actions, modifying my action when they move, how the space between us expands and contracts and how that can move me. It all starts with mindfulness. Am I feeling my legs? Yes. Am I feeling my back? No, feel it. Hard to do. What don't I feel? What do I feel? Touch what I don't feel. Feel it? Yes. And next body part, and on and on as often as possible. For many, their martial art is a conceptual experience rather than a feeling one. If I don't feel me, I can't feel you. If all I feel is you and not me, or not me yet you, then there is no us, no relationship.

The way to realize deep relaxation—in fact, to cultivate relaxation as a way of being—is to continually notice whether or not we are relaxed. Feeling the body as we sit, walk, eat, talk; monitoring the body as whole, or piece by piece. Relaxed arms? Back? Legs? Feet? Face? Etc. The more we do this, the more momentum we build toward being mindful. When mentally upset, feel what being mentally upset is. Stay with the sensation rather than analyze the thoughts. (I make a distinction between sensation or feeling on the one hand, and emotions—which some people also call feelings—on the other. When I say feeling I mean sensation.) It can be hard to stay with sensation when we have so many other things that demand our attention. What I am suggesting is rather than have other things *outside* of feeling our bodies, do these things feeling and with mindfulness: talk to your boss while feeling your body, or shop, or do laundry, drive, whatever. Mindfulness is the foundation of the martial art and the prerequisite to the realization of its principles.

Often I have been told by students that they have a hard time bringing their "mindfulness" into the rest of their lives, particularly work that demands intellectual absorption: working at a computer terminal, operating on a patient, whatever. Deep body awareness takes serious commitment. As I suggested above, pick a part of your body such as your feet. Feel them; do your work; feel them. Do this continually for a period of time, say half an hour. Better still, all the time. Take on more of the body, or a different part the next day. Try the rising and falling of your belly as you breathe. Continually return to sensation upon realization of its lack. I want to emphasize the necessity of experiencing life through our senses. Our intellectual life is critically important and it is a great place to visit, but we don't have to live there. So relax!

To whatever degree you feel yourself, awaken more, go deeper, expand. If our body dies, we are no longer available to act in this reality. Radiate; expand from the body. Do not stop feeling your body in favor of something else.

Feeling

My senses are my connection, my cord to the world. Hearing, seeing, feeling, tasting, smelling—what else is there?

When doing the set (your set), feel the air; give it substance; move the air with you. My teacher has said, "Feel as if you are waist-deep in honey." We drain out of the upper body (draining heaviness) through and around our waist and legs, under our feet. We know we have hands, even with our eyes closed. Good evidence too; we feel them. We don't want to conceptualize our bodies, we want to feel them. I exist because I feel. I would rather "know" I exist because I feel, than have my existence based on a thought. My thoughts of reality are only a description, often an erroneous one.

If I do not feel my back, I do not have the option of moving in that direction. It does not exist for me. I am crippled by my lack of awareness. Since awareness is the realm in which I function, what I am not aware of is forbidden me. Of course there are shades of awareness, hints of intuition, psychic phenomena, different flavors of vision; yet these subtle perceptions should not substitute for more substantial experience.

Full and empty, double-weighted, what do these mean? How do they feel? Maybe there is more to them than what we know, than what we have read. Maybe there is less to them. Would you rather know what full and empty mean or have the skill to accommodate a push or a punch? It is best to have the skill, unless of course I fancy myself a philosopher. Everyone is a philosopher; true skill is rare.

Feel yourself; notice what you feel; maybe it is not a lot, maybe a lot. When I speak of feeling I mean sensation, physical sensation, not labeled sensation like fear or anger, but naked sensation. Anger is a tight chest, band around the forehead; feel the sensation, don't think the sensation. How much of your body do you feel at one time? Notice how the sensation shifts to other parts of the body when you put your attention there. Get clear on what is felt where. I have practiced giving the parts of my body (their depth included) a certain color, say blue, noticing how the color moves and shifts. Then I see if I can fill in the non-colored portions of myself with another color. This enlivens the body and increases the amount of blue. Be creative; make something up to help you feel your whole body. At first it is just pieces. We are moving pieces as our attention moves, so basically we are exercising our attention, making it bigger, increasing its capacity to hold more and more. Experiment with attention "outside" the body and how we lose the body in doing so. As you read this do you feel your feet on the ground, your butt on the chair? Have your body be where you live, not a place you visit when you do T'ai Chi or meditate. This is an ongoing practice and generates its own power and momentum. After all, how can we relax, or sink, if we do not feel what we want to relax or sink? We first have to feel tension to relax, floating to sink.

In T'ai Chi Ch'uan, we speak of power being generated from the ground, given direction through the waist, and expressed through the hands, feet, or whatever we choose to hit or push with. The ground or, closer to us, the feet on the ground, is something felt; if it is not, we cannot distinguish between sinking and floating. If we stop feeling, we are motivated by other considerations and float. The pressure on the bottom of the foot, maintained through the intention and commitment to do so, is connected to the waist through relaxed and springy legs. We have to feel our legs continuously and continuously relax them. Feel them tense, then relax them, over and over again. Feel the pelvis resting on the legs, on the feet, on the ground. If we want to reach out with a hand, turn the pelvis to reach, not the upper body alone to reach. Through feeling this is done, not through thinking is it done. Draining the upper body into the lower, continuously pressing into the ground, feeling if we are draining or not, relaxed or not, pushing off the ground or not—this and not the choreography is T'ai Chi Ch'uan.

In the game of push hands, our awareness and lack of it define our experience, thus our options. If we become involved in using our upper bodies for strength and our arms for pushing, it is often because we do not feel ourselves deeply enough (if at all) to allow for a more relaxed, effortless power. If I feel my whole body, deeply relaxed and resting on the ground, internal power is naturally available; yielding to force is effortless.

Internal martial arts studied mindfully can actually increase our capacity to feel, both in depth and scope. In free play with my teacher I would often realize that he saw things I did not. He responded to things I was not aware of to such a degree that it seemed he was playing a different game than me, in a different arena. When we live in present time we do see more than people who are hypnotized by their own visions and thoughts. Staying with that initial spark, noticing when we are in reaction to the spark, and

41

going "back" into the moment is the discipline. That initial moment is where our "information" lies: where, what, how fast, the intention, etc. Feeling exists only in the moment; the present (energy) recoil is an abstraction.

Many times over the years I have relied on my speed to get me out of the way of a punch or a push. It has the feeling of trying to catch up to what my partner is doing. The punch would be halfway to my face before I would do anything, and then I would quickly dodge or block and cover up. To change this involved a gradual arrival at the realization that I can (and do) feel the immediate environment on the other side of my skin—that the "air" is thick and there is "no space" between me and another or me and the wall. Things have solidity and yet there is space. Solid shadows.

The qualities of the elements can be invoked during a fight or doing sets. The consuming quality of fire, the moving quality of air, the blending quality of water, the solidity of earth. Be careful of course not to confuse what is appropriate with what you think is appropriate.

The danger lies not in our involvement with abstractions but in confusing our abstractions with direct sensual experience. (This is understandable since ultimately there is no separation between observer [senses of observation] and observed.)

In what we can call "mental states" (abstractions, fantasy), again how they are realized is sensual. We hear, feel, taste a good fantasy. The difference is that the fantasy is not perceived through the various sense organs, but is a purely mental event somehow distinct from the "objective" world, where if there is a loud sound, others hear it too.

When faced with an opponent, it is important to be with the situation as is, no more than is necessary added on, either mentally or physically. Whether our attunement is psychic or "physical," we must be engaged with what is before us. Here we find ourselves dodging punches that are not happening or not dodging punches that are, simply because we "are not there" to see what really *is* happening. It can be very entertaining, yet in the "real world" we are getting hit.

The demand on our presence is moment by moment. If I slip into abstraction, even for a flash, it is enough for someone of Peter Ralston's skill to hit me. And when there is pain and fear coming on hard and heavy, the movement towards avoidance is strong.

Being at the center of my awareness means not excluding a particular direction. If we are engaged with something or someone before us, say doing T'ai Chi, sparring, or Aikido with a partner, we do not want to exclude what is at our backs or underneath us. The feeling is more like being immersed in the world rather than inside looking out and seeing spots of the world.

It has often happened that while sitting or simply being mindful enough to notice if something happens to startle me—a car horn honking, the phone going off, anything—I experience the startle itself, which is often a physical jerk, rush, at the instant the startling occurrence happens. It is not a wave that radiates from the event—say the car horn—or that I hear it, then react. There is no gap that would differentiate event and perceiver.

What I am talking about is best exemplified by the old hand-next-to-a-candle experiment. Hold an open hand an inch or so away from a candle, palm facing the side of the flame. Now simply push and pull the flame with your hand. Try abrupt movements, slower movements, different distances. The flame moves with the hand, not after. They seem to be one thing, hand/flame, rather than a hand that makes a flame move. If we choose to feel it, we can have this connection between ourselves and others. When they move we feel them and can be moved with their movement. No gap or

43

separation hinders the unity of the relationship. What separates us are our thoughts about the situation. Our unity is an intrinsic, prior-to-separation "occurrence." In the feeling-sensation realm there is no separation between us and other, us and environment; to the degree we are present and open, we are simultaneous.

What we learn in T'ai Chi Ch'uan is to realize this connection and remain grounded. This gives us the ability to choose how we respond.

Dispassionate Observation

Observing with no attachments to, or investment in, the outcome of an occurrence is dispassionate observation. There is no excess involved. By excess I mean opinions, judgments, meanings.

A person who dispassionately observes another can "sense" another's thoughts and respond accordingly: "If I see the road upon which a man walks I know where he will turn." There is no lag here between thought and occurrence, between the experience of energy and its movement; in fact, there is no emotion.

Change, in all its shapes, is a fundamental truth. That is to say it exists and is continuous, whether or not we as human beings want it to happen (and despite our intentions to manipulate its course). At times it appears to be separate from us; something out there is changing and we are not, or we are changing too slow or too fast and the process is painful. As we live and grow in our lives, change is an ever-present force, appearing sometimes as a friend, at others a foe.

Change can be experienced, and often is, as a source of suffering, a source of pain, whether it is burning your breakfast, getting in a car accident, or the death of a loved one. When change happens, our relationship to it is that of a victim. Or we can be bored, feel as though things are moving too slow, there isn't enough going on, change isn't happening fast enough.

So, things don't happen in the way we want them to or, if they do, it is at the wrong time. People don't act the way we want them to act. When we are in a hurry, all the traffic lights are red. So . . . here we are living our lives, doing our work, being in relationships, all the while buffeted by the winds of change. We would be happy if only things changed the way we wanted them to. The problem with this approach is that it puts the responsibility for our being happy on something we view as separate from ourselves. This is the role of a victim. If we adopt this position it affects (and creates) everything we do, or don't do. We avoid things we think will hurt us, and seek those things that will give us pleasure. This at first glance may appear to be a normal, healthy way to live. Yet, constantly avoiding pain and seeking pleasure can turn into a unsatisfying and unfulfilling game. Even though we may get the new car, or new relationship, or pint of ice cream, we all know that the car will break down, the relationship will change, and the ice cream will soon be gone. Everything changes; change does not stop, it is bigger than we are.

Life is in constant change and is continually making demands. Answer the phone; let out the dogs; buy more ice cream. Whatever. Some demands we like, some we don't. This is the pleasure/pain cycle again; if we get what we want we are happy and we act happy. If we don't, we are unhappy and we act it; in fact, we try to spread it around!

I would like to die awake, to realize my last breath as my last breath. To feel everything, to die and be present for whatever is happening. I would not like to die clutched in fear, anger, mindlessness.

Perception

Consider a punch or a push coming right at you. There is a demand not unlike scraping dog shit off your shoe. You don't like it; you would rather not deal with it; and it won't go away. The difference is you can postpone the shoe cleaning by putting on another pair of shoes. You can't postpone a punch, at least not without getting hit. And sooner or later the shoes will have to be cleaned.

As your intention with the shoe is to clean it, the intention in boxing is to not get hit. Yet although we usually know what to do when an unwanted demand presents itself, there is a lag between the time it does present itself and the time we meet it and take care of it. This lag is often filled with emotional content. In the case of the punch, if there is too long a lag between noticing it and dodging, you get hit; it won't go away even if you get angry at it. Same with the dog shit, a flat tire, or the cold of a Minnesota winter. There is a story of the Zen student who after hearing the miraculous feats of another student's master said, "Yes, my master does miracles, too. When he is hungry he eats, and when he is tired he rests." I don't know if this student's teacher had dogs or studied boxing, but from the story it sounds as though he could handle either.

One fundamental question arises from double practice (push hands, *san hat*, boxing, etc.). How can I keep from becoming competitive when I am doing double practice? Good question. Some people go so far as to say that you cannot box or push hands without being competitive, so it is better not to do it at all. I think this is a very limited point of view, the people adhering to it not ever having experienced being in a "boxing" relationship without also experiencing competition. It most certainly can be done, and be done willfully and consciously.

The experience of loss of self, transcendence, not doing, is common and in fact is a demand in sports or other situations where total presence is required. The experience is one of total absorption in the present situation, so much so that one is no longer self-conscious. The person is no longer experiencing what is happening in a self-conscious way, rather they *are* the experience. There is no longer any room or need for a watcher, someone to watch themselves having an experience. This is a state of being I call "just being" rather than "doing." Doing is trying, making an effort at something, forcing an effect, trying for a desired outcome. There is separation involved in doing, the doer from what he or she is doing. Skiing down a treacherous mountainside, you would allow the mountain to determine where to turn, how to stand, which way to lean; you would be in relationship to the mountain. The same is true in boxing or push hands. Rather than trying to hit your opponent, or trying not to get hit, you would surrender to the situation, accept it as is, without judging or trying to change it; you would allow your partner's punches or push to move you. This is responding appropriately and has nothing to do with me versus you. Competing destroys this relationship and is doing rather than being. Even in punching or pushing your partner, you do so in accordance with what is happening. You punch when your partner offers a "hole" or

48

blank spot in his or her awareness (which manifests in the body). This is an inclusive rather than retaliatory experience.

For any of you who have experienced being the victim of a violent situation, the confusion and the loss of conscious willful action is something that may be hard to forget, and equally hard to clearly remember. The intention of the attacker is not known until too late, and were it known, it would likely not have been responded to appropriately.

Your part of this connection plays a very important role, in that if you express yourself as someone who is not an easy victim, people—including your potential attacker—will pick this up more often than not, and decide they don't want a violent relationship with you.

The best way to respond to an attacker is to respond when they are still a potential attacker. If we are aware of the potential of an attack, we have all the information we need to take the appropriate action to neutralize that potential.

Here we come to the crux of self-defense, and that is (surprise!) awareness. Awareness of your environment, awareness of the people around you, awareness of your body and your attitudes concerning your environment. Awareness of the ground you are standing on.

How you experience the world and how the world experiences you play a fundamental role in your being a victim or not. There is a ceaseless connection evolving between you and the people around you. The dynamics of this connection, such as whether or not violence will occur, are a matter of awareness. Awareness brings choices into play. When there are possibilities of changing your relationship to a potential attacker, such as walking into a grocery store or driving away, by all means do so.

We are not separate from the people we come in contact with; in fact, we have a relationship with everyone in our environment. The degree to which we experience this relationship is a matter of awareness.

Fear, Creating Fear

What are you afraid of . . . right now? If you know . . . that is good; if you don't know, think of something. Something out of the past, or the future. Get some fear going, feel it. Pay attention. . . . Notice how you created your fear. Notice How You Created Your Fear!

Emotions can arise spontaneously in response to a situation rather than an attempt to change the situation. While training to fight in a tournament, a teammate of mine had a sort of breakthrough. He remarked over and over again, "Ya got to fight like you're pissed off." Not to act out, but to embrace the fire of anger and use it to "do your job," which in this case was to win the fight.

When I started the practice of internal martial arts, I had many opportunities to be afraid. I also had the opportunity to study my fear, and studying it I found that it was a constant companion, even outside the context of boxing. I was afraid of not being accepted, of people finding out I was afraid of not being accepted; I was afraid of getting hurt, of being clumsy, of not having enough money, of getting fired, on and on.

Peter Ralston has said, "To the degree we are present, there is no fear." Fear always has its foundation in a prior or future event. It originates as a concept. We can tighten up, hold our breath, physically shut down, get uptight, whatever. Fear is a workable arena in which to discover sensation and to practice mindfulness. For instance, we can lose our thoughts and just feel—directly access our senses. This gives us more options; now we are in contact—physical contact— with our environment. We don't want to become lost in our reaction to a fantasy, getting tenser, reinforcing our thoughts about our "dangerous situation."

One of the most crippling of reactions we can have to anything is to check out, go away, space out, wish we weren't there. When we are in danger, being present with the situation and being in one's body is the best strategy for survival; if not, we cut ourselves off from the very information needed to deal with the situation appropriately.

Many times I had the opportunity to cross the Mississippi, walk across on a two-foot-wide plank supplied with a loose cable as a hand rail. Now two feet is pretty wide, and the plank was sturdy and also seventy-five feet above the river, a crossing easily handled by someone who has trained for many years in the martial arts. I would not do it. The bottom fell out when the bridge left the ridge. The ground five feet away was replaced by rocks at the bottom fifty feet away. I felt the space between me and the river. I hit my hands and knees and crawled back to safety.

When I am at the edge of a cliff or a tall building ledge, my attention leaps over the side. My body follows my attention, so a struggle starts. If I feel my back and fill out the space behind me with as much attention as I am putting into the drop before me, the situation becomes workable. If I feel my feet on the ground in the middle of my experience, I know where I stand . . . where I am. Often in T'ai Chi push hands it is a discipline not to overreach with our attention in one direction while sacrificing our sense of stability (groundedness). Many times I have seen students reach too far and lose their balance when trying to find their partner's balance.

Let us order the stages of development:

- Form: here one learns technique, shapes to take, rules to obey.

- Surrender: here one learns to yield to demands, to surrender their position, their form of mind.

51

- Transcendence: here one becomes inclusive of duality. One experiences "no judging"; Wu Wei, just being. One expands their experience of the world to include "other." One assumes responsibility.

- Devotion: devotion is being committed to the truth.

These are in order not chronologically but as an expanding experience. In fact, each stage can flow into and out of the others. They are often intertwined, creating one's consciousness and a map of one's mind. Also, these stages are circular in experience. For example, now I am experiencing the pain of surrendering to a new form; growth demands surrender. Someday I will transcend the form I have built. As this expands I will feel full, on my path . . . and then changes will come about and what I am doing will be restricting. If I defend my position rather than surrender and expand, I will suffer (devotion turning into defense); if I surrender and "die" I will suffer . . . but I will find a new path and myself in my new experience and feel full again.

Before trying to manipulate a situation into something else, one must always experience it exactly as it is. As the situation changes one must be with, and open to, what is now. Skill in boxing does not come from any effort to do the right thing at the right time, but rather from surrendering to the demands and allowing them to determine your actions. One must always include their partner in their experience.

There is an integrity to this art that transcends personality or conscious self-experience. There is no room for thoughts; the experience is full, no gaps in time or awareness. There is no relationship, no you and no them.

Natural intelligence must command your actions. This is divine boxing.

Ego

We seem to be in the middle, "between" intending to relax and allowing relaxation.

Is there non-conceptual intending? Can we eat without an intention, or a concept of doing so, or would we miss our mouth? What is a word, a pen, a language, illumination? Is it possible that conceptual mind is essential to human experience?

The first noble truth in Buddhism is Suffering. That is our basic condition. The third noble truth is the cessation of suffering, that it is possible for suffering to end. This cessation is often described as a non-conceptual "way of being." Without a sense of self wouldn't we be . . . ineffectual, to say the least?

I realize that a sense of self receives a bad rap in certain circles; yet try to do something, anything (except non-rem sleep) without it. If you could, that would be non-rem sleep.

The texts of the Vajrayana tradition of Buddhism describe a way of being as direct experience—nonconceptual direct experience. This is having experience through sight, hearing, tasting, smelling, feeling, with no reflection on or concept of the experience. As we experience directly, this state of being shifts immediately to experience based on inference and concept. Our being flickers between the two so fast, so subtly, that most of us confuse the two. What we see has meaning, meaning we give it, as if the meaning is intrinsic. This is how we construct our experience. Through the practice of moment-by-moment awareness we acquire the freedom of choice that awareness naturally allows.

Destroying the ego is something I have heard about for many years. In fact, I have spent years believing that it is the noblest act we can perform as humans. Now I am not so sure. First, I am not so sure it can be done, and second, I don't know what would be left and if it would be workable.

Ego is our location of self; who we think we are, who we are. It is the collection of sense perceptions and mental activity that together equals an identity. Without the ability (gift or curse?) to distinguish, to see and act, to create boundaries, it would be impossible to function. Without the ability to perceive self and other, the hand from the tree, the phone book from the sink, there would be no hands, trees, sinks, or phone books.

Is there self without something to compare something else to? I have had experiences that appeared selfless, unbounded; and yet at the same time there was awareness. There was no monitoring or judging of what was perceived. There was a watcher but no one watching the watcher.

Our separateness is not the source of our suffering, it is our not liking what we see. It is our wanting things to stay the same or to be different than they are. Without separateness there would be no appreciation. Consider the phrase, "You are beautiful to me." To realize the difference between "what is" and "what isn't" is the discriminating wisdom of a warrior.

We all have a tendency to see things, events, whatever, in such a way that we take stuff out, add other stuff, see some things, yet miss others. What we do see we judge, ponder, emote about. When playing push hands, or boxing, or whatever, it is to our advantage to see the event clearly, without bias. This quality—"to see things as they are"—is the goal of spiritual practice.

The seeming contradiction between boundaries and no boundaries is irrelevant. "We" have an intelligence that can function—and in fact is determined by—the nonconceptual reality of the moment. This intelligence is immediate in its capacity and design. It is not observing an event *per se*. The "observed" and "observer" are arising together, and within this "realm" of mutual arising, amazingly, we have the capacity to act. We can even deny intrinsic intelligence and live our lives in a conceptual dreamland. But we can choose.

Because of the broad and encompassing quality of our naked awareness, in moments of truth and unquestioned movement the ability to identify distinctions is at once rendered meaningless and unmistakable. There is no confusion concerning the logistics (what, where, whom, when, etc.) of the given situation. Our course of action is restricted only by our immediate limitations, our lack of awareness.

Which of the realms we are currently engaged in makes a lot of difference in our ability to do martial arts. It is through mindfulness that we realize what we are doing. When, for example we are practicing leading and a separation occurs, it is often because we pull away or want our partner to go where he doesn't want to. When we do this we present to our partner a gap in our mindfulness, a gap manifested on a somatic level.

Groundedness

A long with the relaxation and effortless movement gained through being aligned with gravity, we use gravity pressing us to the ground as the source of our power.

In my experience, as we participate in being caught between gravity pushing us down and the earth holding us up—by participate I mean "relax as surrender" to it—we immediately become more grounded and our tissues change. They become less woody and more rubbery—at first a soft rubber, then gradually denser. This rubbery quality of the tissues is intrinsic; we don't make it happen, we just relax. If we tense, the rubber turns to wood. That is called external strength. It is internal strength (or intrinsic strength) that is trained in the practice of internal martial arts.

We don't "do" the power. We set it up through proper alignment, body mechanics, and logistics (timing, distance, etc.). What we "do" is relax and compress. Only a relaxed muscle will compress. The power that moves us and/or the person we push (uproot) or hit—whatever—is available because we are relaxed and compressed, aligned with gravity. It is not because we use muscular contraction, exertion. Our partner bounces off us because we move into them; we don't push them out and away from us. We need not do any more movement than is required to perform this function.

While the flexing muscles are contracting, the extensor muscles should be relaxed, and vice versa. It is not to our advantage to have one set of muscles in competition with another.

We need to intend to be grounded. With our intention we feel plugged into the ground and can move from there. We maintain our intention to be relaxed. Most of us have a lot of momentum towards being tense, which is ungrounded. The practice is to know what we are doing and return not only to relaxation but to openness and groundedness.

Groundedness is what naturally happens when we allow ourselves to relax. Relaxation opens boundaries. We feel more, so more information is available to us. *Being grounded keeps us from becoming overwhelmed.*

Feel everything—the body, the space inside the body, the deep breath, the flesh, the movement, the ebb and flow of attention as it moves, the skin, all that is available through the senses of hearing, sight, smell, and taste, the mental event of our being, our reactions, judgments, or particular style or attitudes of openness and holding. Stand aligned with the most available and unbroken force of our existence; stand to allow it to press the body into your feet. Relax; surrender to gravity; cultivate a feeling of draining into the earth beneath your feet. Remain or become lighter, more diffuse in your upper body, denser and compressed in your legs and feet. The pressure of your upper body then rests on top of your lower. Any movement originates from the pressure where the feet meet the ground. Use that pressure to move the body; to move a hand, use the ground; to turn the waist, use the ground; for direction use the waist. Being physically pressed to the ground by gravity, we are squeezed between heaven and earth; the more we relax and surrender to gravity, the more power is available to us. We can shine with it. To reach out and touch we do not reach up; we do not push ourselves away from the pressure we have allowed through our surrender to gravity. Stable in our position, not depending on what we touch to hold us up, not unsettling ourselves when we miss, we touch from the pressure at our feet.

We are caught, held between two great forces: gravity and the ground. We are constantly being pressed (the one force) against the other by gravity. Without the ground to prevent it, we would be in free fall, in a state of no gravity until we met the ground. Without the ground to support us, we would not even experience gravity. Of course, if we were in free fall we would be buffeted by the wind coming up to meet us. If we didn't know any better we would be motionless with wind surging upwards from below.

Stand; bend your knees; drop your pelvis; breathe in your belly; put yourself over your feet; feel yourself aligned with gravity; shift your weight sixty-forty percent to one foot, gravity pushing you into both your feet. Relax, soften. Raise an arm—either arm—and drain any heaviness into your feet, feel gravity pressing you against the ground and drain, drop any heaviness in the upper body into the lower and put it on the ground. Feel it in the pressure where your feet meet the ground. Put a small object in your raised hand and feel the addition of weight on the ground, in your weighted foot. You are pressed between gravity pushing you against the ground and the "ground pushing back" (every force equal and opposite), squeezed between gravity and the ground. Feel the pressure of the object in your hand compressing you further. Feel pressed between the object in your hand and the ground. Like a basketball. Feeling this makes intrinsic power available to you. Relaxing enough to allow your muscles to compress, and feeling this as the case, is the key to manifesting this type of internal power. Simply knowing how to do it isn't it.

"Bottoming out" is what I call resting on full compressed legs. *Chin* (or intrinsic strength) is used to move, whether shifting our weight from foot to foot, stepping, turning the waist, striking, or pushing. Once we have a workable practice of Chin—when it is real and we know how we do it—any shape can be taken; form is secondary. In my opinion, getting intrinsic power down is primary; it is what makes the art an internal art. Draining, compression, relaxation, alignment with gravity—the principles are the foundation of the practice.

If I hit a basketball with my fist coming straight down on top of it, my fist will bounce off. The "straight down" is very important. My fist on top of the ball, the ground on the bottom, the ball is compressed and my fist bounces. In a punch I am the basketball and I "throw myself" at my target and am compressed between the pressure at the end of my fist (impact) and the ground at my feet. My target bounces away, or moves, or says ouch! The hitting straight down is akin to us standing aligned with gravity. If we hit the ball at an angle there will still be a bounce, yet greatly diminished. The ball, not being compressed squarely against the ground, will bounce away. If we are not aligned with gravity, our power is greatly diminished and we either bounce off our target, crumple, or tense up just to keep standing. Tense muscles have little resiliency and do not compress well.

We can also bounce our partner off his legs by pressing him into the ground. This can be done with a push (uproot), punch, kick, shoulder, or whatever we want.

When I strike, I am "caught," squeezed between the pressure met at the end of my fist and the pressure at the ground, at my feet. If there are gaps between, places not felt, not supported from below, or the structure is not aligned to allow pressure atop to reach the feet, the resulting break will add a muscular tension needed to support the structure.

Maintaining this "attitude" of surrender and connection with the ground is of number-one importance. It cannot be done without the committed "practice" of awareness. Only with awareness can the habitual tendencies to react, to push away, to retaliate be replaced with allowance, acceptance, and the deep power needed to invoke new qualities. Talking oneself into it does not work; "working on it" is often an excuse not to do it when you are not working on it.

There are practices of bodywork that train the human structure to exist with the constant power of gravity in the most efficient manner; that is, to stand aligned with, rather than struggling against, gravity. The vertebrae are stacked like coins, the pelvis dropped (relaxed not pulled), the sacrum pressing into the heel (this is a feeling sense), and the pubic bone into the ball of the foot. Knees bent, bottomed out, draining.

I learned this goal in bodywork and as a principle of T'ai Chi Ch'uan simultaneously. The difference is that in bodywork someone else does it to you. When we get Rolfed, the Rolfer will stretch, lengthen, balance our bodies, getting us aligned with gravity. In T'ai Chi Ch'uan we do it ourselves.

Getting Rolfed is a process that takes weeks. T'ai Chi Ch'uan can take years. Years are going to pass anyway. Two years from now we will be two years older and we could be a two-year-old T'ai Chi player/veteran. To the degree we bring awareness into both approaches, to that degree the benefits deepen. Personally, I believe without a practice of mindful movement like T'ai Chi, Feldenkrais, or something, simply receiving tablework has a very short-lived effect.

61

It is important to bring what is learned on the table into our lives, or the old habits that twisted and bent our bodies in the first place will simply twist and bend them again. Without awareness and responsibility we will not heal.

Sinking

Here I must introduce another piece of the picture, a location in the body which in Chinese is called the Tan Tien; in Japanese, Hara. I will refer to it as "center." It is a point two or three fingers' width below the navel, and it is from here that we give the power, which is rooted in the feet, direction or a place to go.

Let your mind and attention fall into the center. From this place there is a direct connection with the world. It is simple and has no confusion. One can actually feel the "outside" world from this part of the body. A natural intelligence resides there.

Now the weight must be placed mostly on one foot; personally I prefer about eighty percent on one leg, twenty percent on the other (what I am discriminating here is torso weight). Both legs should be relaxed and resting on the ground. This brings us to another aspect of the manifestation of Chin, which is filling and emptying. Both legs are relaxed; yet one is supporting the majority of the body's weight, the other is merely relaxed and resting on the ground. In actuality both are relaxed; yet one is full, the other empty. How can one stand on relaxed legs? As the amount of muscular contraction used in holding yourself up is diminished, it is replaced by an actual feeling of filling in the legs.

Stand on the ground; feel your weight on the ground, the pressure on the bottom of your feet. Relax. Throw open your joints—all your joints—let your pelvis drop into alignment with gravity; don't push or pull anything. Soften your tissues; in order to do this you have to feel your tissues, your skin, your muscles, fascia, organs, blood. Relax everything and stand aligned with gravity, everything falling and relaxing into your feet. Relax your mind; let your attention rest on what is happening. When it wanders bring it back; don't fight, just bring it back. The more we relax and fall into our feet, the more potential we have for Chin.

So, here we are standing on the ground feeling relaxed, sunk, and aligned with gravity. What we want to do now is move. Remember, how we do that is by using the pressure we have on the ground as the source of our power, and connecting it to our center.

We want to stand on our legs as if they were two balloons. Whether full of air or empty, a balloon is not contracting or holding itself in any way. When filled, it simply forms itself around the air inside it. The balloon itself is relaxed, though stretched; it isn't fighting itself or the air inside. The air does the work; the balloon is relaxed. We can compare the air to Ch'i, compressed air to stored Chin. So with compressed air inside the balloon, the potential for power is cultivated. The balloon is full; so are we, pressed on the ground by gravity, our tissues relaxed and full.

Now it is rather obvious that a balloon with a leak in it would constantly need refilling and would not be able to focus all its energy in one direction. For example, if you blew up a leaky balloon and let go of it without tying the end, it would not fly through the air as swiftly or as committedly as a balloon with no leaks. Its power would be split. So in our bodies we must feel the whole as one piece with our attention on ourselves and our life force at this present moment. Only then can we participate in energetic reality. No matter the technique used to get in touch with energy, the underlying thread and prerequisite is to be present, now. Energy only exists in the present; if your attention is elsewhere you will miss it!

To deliver a blow or take a step, the whole body must be comprehended as a unit with no gaps between the pressure on the ground and its outward manifestation. Do not be confused; this is actually a rather simple thing to do, although it demands deep and true experience. Remember that our source of power is the earth, and the earth will bestow its power on anyone who surrenders to it. There is no tension or muscular contraction in any part of the body at any time. This is an essential ingredient. Even when throwing a punch there is no muscular exertion. Your tissues and joints are open and relaxed, manifesting the ground or the pressure on the bottom of your full foot in your hands. In fact, one must drain and sink one's feeling attention into the feet, making the upper body subservient to the lower. The power residing in your root is given direction by your center and intention by your mind. Again, do not be confused; mind, body, energy are not separate. Only for clarification and study should they be viewed separately.

This way of being—relaxed, sunk, unified, aligned with gravity, weighted on mostly one foot—is our foundation in the internal martial arts. All these parts must be experienced and manifested together and at the same time. From here we can listen to and interpret another's energy.

Remember, when uprooting we do not push our partner away from us; rather we allow their weight to compress us and (we) bounce them away.

Differentiate between strength and power. If there is a

struggle, you are probably double-weighted. Be patient and "hold" your partner's weight. This is done with feeling. As usual, differentiate between moving sensation and moving meat. We want to be with each movement from its beginning to end and into the next . . . almost as if there is no next, just the big movement. Many times we start a movement, like a pulse, then we space out, go away; maybe we come back at its completion. Nobody is home in all that intervening time.

I think it was Yang Cheng Fu, a T'ai Chi heavyweight (literally and figuratively), who said that we want to relax to the point of feeling invisible. Sure, most of us think we have to hold on, keep it together or else we will fall apart, but in my experience when our bodies change so does the way we see, think, and respond to the world around us. When we deeply relax, some things may fall apart, maybe some old crusty viewpoints and ideas. Get loose and be open to whatever comes along and you will become perennially relaxed and open.

If we relax we are sunk. We are constantly being met by the force of gravity. If we stop pushing against it and allow ourselves to be pressed against the ground and feel it press us to the ground (participate in it), we are sunk.

In our relationship to gravity we want to be like a diver slicing through water. No bellyflopping. If we hold ourselves at a tilt, that is, if we are leaning in one direction or the other, we have to use effort—and it is usually chronic effort—to keep ourselves from falling over. If we are leaning we cannot relax, because if we did, again gravity would pull us off our feet to the ground. Relaxing, sinking, standing aligned with gravity with your pelvis dropped will allow compression.

Breath can be used to increase that pressure as it moves down and into the pelvic dish and into the perineum. Such breathing also fills the middle body, ming it up, so to speak, so no leaks or breaks can occur. A leak or a break is anywhere the body is mechanically not aligned with gravity, causing musculature alone to hold it up. Rather, we want to relax and fall into the feet. A leak that separates upper and lower can simply be not feeling, or having an empty solar plexus. In the Cheng Man-Ch'ing style of Yang T'ai Chi, the pressure in the perineum is accomplished by inhaling into it. Whenever we want to hit or push or kick—or whatever demands power (even moving)—we inhale into and fill the lower abdomen. There are schools of T'ai Chi that accomplish similar results by doing what is called opposite breathing. On the inhale the abdomen contracts; exhaling it expands. On the punch there is an exhale pressing into the perineum. More than just inhaling down, the abdomen fills on the sides, back and up against the diaphragm; as if there is a basketball in the belly, it expands in all directions. In my opinion the breath is something to play around with. At first breathe deeply and naturally in the belly. Trying to exhale every time one does a push or punch in the T'ai Chi set will simply make you dizzy. With time the breath, as used for more power, will become the natural thing to do, but without proper body mechanics it is pretty worthless. After we internalize the body mechanics, breath is a powerful and important next step.

Relax, soften
Align with gravity
Drain
Compress
Unify
Sacrum in heel
Pelvis dropped
Breathe in the belly

Wu Wei
T'ai Chi Ch'uan

Wu Wei T'ai Chi Ch'uan is the essence. It is the study of ourselves, our bodies, our relationship to others and to our environment, physically and energetically. Truthfully it is not a study of shapes, forms, and techniques, but rather the experience of the source from which the shapes and forms arise. It is primordial and simple.

Here I must differentiate between what is and what isn't. Anything experienced outside the present, that isn't happening right here and now, isn't. It does not exist in energetic reality.

Truth, reality exist now. There is no struggle, no contest; there is simply moving with what is.

In the context of T'ai Chi Boxing there is also no fight, no struggle. This is my experience from light play to the heat of combat. Whether I am dodging a punch or throwing a punch, my actions are determined by my partner's actions. This demands total immersion in the moment and unity with my partner.

Many people believe that practicing the self-defense aspects of T'ai Chi Ch'uan spurs competitiveness and aggression. Quite to the contrary, I think it is the perfect environment in which to study and experience fear and competitiveness because it is an environment where these arise. Surely to have the ability to make choices around fear and competition one must be able to face them directly. When competition and aggression arise out of the practice, they should be acknowledged and that energy returned to the present moment where there is no separation and no fear.

To avoid our fear and aggression by avoiding situations that will "push our buttons" is literally avoidance. To be calm in the midst of chaos cannot be accomplished by avoiding chaos. I have a choice concerning aggression and combat and I can choose from my heart, not out of fear. To live in fear is to live in avoidance. Instead we want to jump into life, become immersed in it.

Wu Wei is most often translated as non-action, or notdoing. It does not mean "doing nothing." One of the best examples is flowing water. At various points along a stream, the water can be still, effervescent, moving fast or slow, gurgling or silent. There is a lot of action, constantly changing, but always it is just water. It is being "moved" by the forces of nature according to its own intrinsic water-ish-ness. I doubt very much that the still water wishes and hopes that it will someday move swiftly. I also doubt that it is jealous of the mobility and apparent freedom of the clouds above it. There is nothing added on, there are no hollows or projections; it is manifesting its true nature. If the water were jealous of the clouds or if it decided when and where to gurgle or be still, then it would be doing. My guess is that then it would also realize struggle, pain, and suffering.

Consider ourselves. We are sentient beings in relationship with other sentient beings—going to work, eating and drinking, making love, paying the bills, etc. Within all of this "activity," how much time do we spend struggling and suffering and being offended by what the world (other) does to us? What, truly, are the motives for what we do in our lives? I heard once that the Chinese character "surrender" also means "to perish." Like water perhaps, or fast downhill skiing, or boxing, or going to work? I can't really "perish"; I have bills to pay, my reputation to live up to. How are we to live?

Living in the "experience" of not-knowing (or Wu Wei) demands sober investigation into the source of our being, of who we are. Just who is studying T'ai Chi? Who is reading this? How do you know? Do you know?

Being open to possibilities frees us from our own encumbering thoughts of ourselves and the world in which we live. Our experience is fresh and new, moment to moment, rich with potential, open to change.

The "way" of not-knowing has more a flavor of possibilities than knowing. It has an openness to things-as-they-are instead of a knowledge of them. I am going to give an example here; the "activity" is downhill skiing. I have never downhill-skied so I am going to fake it.

You are going skiing at your favorite resort and your favorite hill. You have skied this hill say, hundreds of times, all hours of day, under all sorts of climatic conditions. It is a big hill, and a fast one. You get set, put your gear on, go to the hill; you're ready to go for it. You *know* that hill; you know how it will feel to go down it; you know which way you will go; you know every bump and tree. Let me interrupt here; this is the time, at the top of the hill ready to go down, when it would be best to let go of knowing and become open to possibilities. But let's say you don't. You start, you build up speed, maybe a little faster than you should but you know the trail, and you know what is ahead until . . . until . . . Oh Gawd! Where did that tree come from???

Consider driving a car; consider riding a bike; consider a walk in the woods; consider boxing. Chances are very good that we have all, at times, come from not-knowing, from

71

being open to possibilities. Which way of being do we come from in our practice of T'ai Chi Ch'uan?

Wu Wei Ch'uan is about freedom manifested through conscious relationship with another person. This freedom demands deep consideration of what is going on. We no longer choose to act outside this experience of relationship. Doing so promotes a powerful me-versus-them attitude towards people (or situations) that tries to take our freedom away. It substitutes another "feeling," one dependent upon external factors, things separate from us, out there. It is a "freedom" that needs protecting, a "freedom" we are afraid of losing.

The open freedom of Wu Wei is no longer dependent on the circumstances of our lives. This freedom cannot be taken away and is inclusive of other people and the world around us. Yet it is a freedom steeped in paradox, a freedom that must be directly experienced to be realized. When we realize it, there are no longer any "enemies" out there. The world is taken and accepted at face value, realistically. There is the clear, naked acceptance of a warrior, and one's life is empowered because in this freedom our experience is always one of choice. Nothing needs protecting; there is no longer a fight, for one is not acting out of a separate sense of self. Rather we begin to experience being in relationship, constantly, moment by moment. Wisdom and compassion guide our behavior, rather than fear and protection.

Thinking, Doing, and Wu Wei

Do not focus on a piece of what is going on. Feel your whole body; feel the space around your body as well as what is going on in front of you. Feel your partner's body and the space around it. Feel the two of you and the space around and between, like two parts of one body. Fill the space between you with feeling pressure.

Cultivate groundedness rather than assume what you think is a grounded shape. Feel the ground; relax and stand aligned with gravity. To stay grounded when moving (rather than adhering to the choreography of someone who is grounded), feel plugged into the earth, relaxed, and draining into the feet, aligned with gravity. Explore how to get from one foot to the other without pushing off the ground and thus severing your root.

Adults have been doing what they do for many years. If graced with a healthy body, we have been walking, running, shifting our weight from foot to foot, standing on one leg, playing balancing games our whole lives . . . since childhood. When we are learning a martial art this skill is not to be ignored. In favor or not, personal style is a gift if it is not used as an excuse to avoid more open ways of being.

When teaching, I look at what someone does that works —whatever it is, by principle or not—and I support it. I also try to encourage common sense and discovery when the actions are "inappropriate." Shaming is not my style.

We naturally move very powerfully as anyone (like me) who has walked into a table or missed the door can tell you. People study martial arts for years trying to cultivate that kind of power.

Technique

We want to see things as they are, that is, with naked awareness—no judging, no importance, no meaning. A punch needs to be dodged; a push needs to be neutralized. We create the intention to blend, yield, attack, yet do so in accordance with real conditions.

We live and train a paradox: no planning, judging, yet sustaining intention; maintaining an openness to things with no plan of manipulation to make us feel safer or stronger. We hold the intention to mold ourselves around the activity of our partner and use that activity to our advantage. When our partner is vulnerable—we attack; where they don't see—we go; our activity is directed only by them.

When boxing (or dancing) we can feel "space" between each other; rather than depend solely on sight to dodge a punch, we feel it. We feel it starting at its creation and blend with that, then. Any sense of rushing around disappears. We will have plenty of time to do . . . whatever. At Peter Ralston's school I have done simple exercises around this theme. Mirroring another, one person moves and the other follows. Initially it is sight that allows the game; yet with openness and study, feeling starts to mirror.

To be moved by your partner is what we strive for and, as he or she moves, openings and closings are constantly acknowledged and used. If the game is boxing, we use them to our advantage. As I stand before a mirror and hold my hands up and in front of me as if I were boxing, there are places on my body that would be more accessible than others. If I "take another stance" the same would be true, differently. If I move around and shadowbox, the same would be happening but in a constant shifting pattern. Yet the total square inches of available body to be struck and the total square inches that are harder to get at don't vary.

By flowing with our partner, surrendering to his movement and sticking to it, we fill in our partner's "holes" and acknowledge his fullness. We acknowledge his fullness by filling in his holes. This is obviously not something which is restricted to a particular martial art, or even to the martial arts.

In the midst of our surrender we need to acknowledge the game. We need to hold and maintain the intention to play. This is a place where paradox arises. To realize boundaries while deeply surrendering to a lack of boundaries can seem contradictory. Surrender is a surrender of boundaries—physical and mental—to feeling our partner; feeling his body, his intention and attitude. What arises through the act of surrender is realized and molded to accomplish a goal. Do you get my point? Surrender = no boundaries; intention = boundaries.

What arises through our surrender is used, in a way that does not corrupt the act of surrender, to our advantage.

In martial arts it is very important to be in relationship, to flow with your partner, moment by moment, and to realize whenever you are no longer present. Then, without any judging, jump back into it. Vipassana Martial Arts! A workable wielding of Manjushri's blade.

It is very easy, especially if we know the choreography of the practice, to replace being with our partner in a feeling-oriented way with a more conceptually oriented attitude. We know what our partner is going to do next, or how he should respond to our technique, and that is the way we treat the situation. As if we really know. . . .

If we can see our partner's adding or subtracting to or from the situation, we want to move and act in ways that encourage his confusion, "confusion" being his not knowing the difference between what is actually happening and what he thinks is happening.

Often just touching my partner will start him going: "He is touching my shoulder; I have to do something." Actually my touch is not a threat. Yet he focuses on the touch, often to the exclusion of the rest of his body, and makes a plan, then tries to carry it out. I touch, he reacts, and while he is forming and becoming involved with his plan I go else-where. This can be done with very small movements on my part; yet my partner is in a constant state of trying to adjust, focused on catching up. (This can often be accomplished with stepping.) In order for me to keep someone off balance in this way I have to see what my partner sees. If I want my partner to react to something I do, he has to see what I do, and I have to see him see it, to continue leading his atten-tion. I have to see what he is attending to. If the donkey doesn't see the carrot, the donkey won't follow. Some people need larger, more obvious carrots than others; we do what is required. The information comes from our partner, we mold to him.

Shortly after I started studying with Peter Ralston, we (Peter and I) played (boxed) and he noticed my pride in my kicking skill and remarked, "You've done Tae Kwon Do, right?" With stepping he then effectively cut any potential I had to hit him with a kick. He was seeing my intention, my plan, and keeping me in the formulation stage of throwing a kick. He simply did not offer himself as a target that could be kicked. He saw what I wanted and led me with it, offering and taking away, all determined by me.

If we are not participating in a relationship and our partner has a deeper, more true experience than we do, we will lose in boxing, or more importantly, in a serious fight we don't want to lose.

When I used to box with Peter, he would quickly and impactfully fill any holes I would open. The reason was not necessarily his superior technique but his quality of presence and willingness to play the game. This was a game in which, when the going got rough, the willingness to be there and deeply feel your own experience "as is" became increasingly hard to do. Our tendency when "confronted" with pain— either the pain of getting hit or the pain of unwillingness to play (any game)—is immediately to jump into our well-practiced and often entrenched sense of defending ourselves, our position, or to space out. Boxing or playing push hands with Peter made it very clear to me, over and over, that at least in my relationship to Peter, denial didn't work and was a great hindrance. It was also simply bad strategy. Supporting and taking advantage of our partner's denial is good strategy. That is especially true if we are playing a game where it is to our advantage to win. For those of us who have been in loving relationships (all of us), there is obviously much more going on than taking the advantage and winning.

Behind every technique is the purpose of the technique. While training, this crucial element must not be forgotten. Every situation is ongoing and ever-changing. Sacrificing purpose for technique is a common mistake.

Even when practicing solo sets, being purposeful, powerful, yet open to self-examination and exploration are trained through the study of technique. When in relationship, how we are with our partner—scared or not, powerful or not, present or not, feeling or not—is a training of awareness. A training of awareness provides an excellent means of feedback.

The centerline is a notion that is important in many martial arts. It is basically the line that runs down the center of our bodies. When we are parrying punches, the centerline is something not to go beyond. That is, we don't need to push our partner's punch past where it is rendered useless. That distinction of distance can be very small. In a more feeling arena, the centerline is that core of the body around which we rotate when we turn the pelvis, whether to dodge a punch, yield to a push, or whatever. In the game of two-person work the centerline is what we should seek out in our partner. It is often felt as a core which many people have a hard time yielding. Particularly in push hands it is the target.

For example, if I would push my partner's shoulder he could simply turn his (her) waist to yield (right shoulder pushed, turn the pelvis to the right). This would work as long as the push was in a straight line. If the push were a train, the turning of the pelvis would be jumping off the tracks. If I pushed on the center of my partner's chest, simply turning his own pelvis would not do the trick. Yielding demands participation by the person being pushed in the push. Rather than go into reaction, we actually participate. We blend; then we lead. In the case of a partner aiming for our center we need to blend. In yielding and blending we always move in the same direction and at the same speed as the push; later we can create the "gap" necessary to create a new line.

The centerline is what we want to keep elusive. We can bait with it (lead) by letting our partner feel it. An extraordinary quality (that can be trained) is the movement of the centerline. We can rotate around our centerline whether it is located centrally or on the left or right half of our body. It is the *feeling* of centerline that is important. If pushed in the center of the chest we can, with feeling, move the core around—we rotate to the left or right of that and swing open like a door on our off-center centerline to accommodate the push.

By touching someone on the shoulder, on the chest, anywhere, we want to feel the core—their centerline—and adjust the angle, speed, and depth of our push to accommodate our partner's trying to keep his center from being caught. If we miss his center it is much easier for him to yield. Often our partner's resistance will lead us directly to his center.

"Leading" is allowing your partner to follow you as a target. Specifically, we offer a piece of ourselves. In push hands we can offer an arm or shoulder, etc., to be pushed; in boxing we offer any available target. "Available" is the central issue in leading. The target must be made so attractive to the attacker, the attacker would rather attack the target we offer than anything else. It is the easiest place to hit. If the target we offer is not attractive and available, the attacker will simply not go for it but attack elsewhere. If our target is out of range, or if our intention to lead is detected by our partner, he simply won't go there. If the partner pulls away from our leading we "simply" see his new target, we see what he wants and lead with that. *So we can only lead an attacker where he or she wants to go.*

If our relationship is adversarial, that is, if we oppose the wishes of our partner, then we cannot blend with him. I only weigh 130 pounds. It is not to my advantage to oppose the wishes of a 200-pounder. In our partner's moving and reaching for a target, he often neglects other variables, say, his own balance. By leading we can pull our partner off balance, cause him to step awkwardly, put him in positions whereby he is available to being pushed or thrown. We may choose to simply let his fire burn itself out by not letting him hurt us and not hurting. Maybe he will wake up.

Double-weightedness is often spoken of as simply having one's weight evenly distributed on both feet. In every T'ai Chi set I have ever seen, double-weightedness only occurs, if at all, at the beginning and end of the set.

The arguments against double-weightedness include an inability to yield, an equal inability to step, a vulnerability to being uprooted, and less power. All are partially true. Basically what I recommend is that you investigate it on your own. If you simply believe me, that's all your correction of double-weightedness will be: a belief. A more subtle quality of double-weightedness is simply (profoundly) using another person to support our weight, to keep us from losing our balance. If I throw a punch or push at you, and you dodge it, and because of my miss I am thrown (throw myself) off balance, my punch has a quality of double-weightedness. If I lean on you, giving my weight to you in such a way that if you suddenly disappeared I would fall, my leaning is double-weighted. Reaching for a target (any target) in such a way that you move your balance away from your base and fall is double-weighted. This is a quality of relationship that obviously is not confined to martial arts. We leave our center. A relationship in which another is needed to support our balance is double-weighted. If we do not support our own weight, we become our own opponent. A balanced opponent merely has to move to dislodge us.

In push hands we want to displace our partner's center (space) with ours. After we find his center, which is one of the components of the push hands game, we can uproot our partner unless he yields to our push. At that moment we do not want to find ourselves double-weighted and involved in a struggle to correct our balance. We want to be stable, balanced, and participating in the game of finding our partner's weight (center) and keeping our own weight unavailable to him.

Remember. We can grab our partner's attention at times by simply touching him. Touch draws attention like a magnet.

We want to grab or catch our partner's attention and then simply attack where his attention is lacking. We get our partner to focus his attention on whatever it is we want him to. Another way of proceeding is to notice what our partner is already focused on—the target we put before him perhaps, perhaps not—and go from there. We attack what he doesn't see; consequently the attack is often missed by him because his attention is focused on something else. As our partner adjusts, or reacts to our attack (focuses on it), we move elsewhere; we attack where he doesn't see, on and on, until he is defeated. We seem to be always ahead; he is reacting, trying to "catch up" to what is going on.

When leading, stay attached to your partner. You have a direct antenna to his next intention. If your partner's hands are on your body or arms, do not give him reason to put them elsewhere. When your partner pushes or yields, respond in such a manner that makes his hands the wake behind your lead. The lead (boat) and *the wake it creates* cannot be separated.

In presenting ourselves as the target, we open ourselves to intimate participation in the relationship. If someone is in a position, and properly distanced, with intent to throw a punch, you see that person in his position and distanced, with intent to throw a punch. You don't see the punch and you don't behave as though a punch is happening. That way, when the punch happens you see it as it is. You see its trajectory, its power, its limit, and because you are cool while you participate, you move out of the way. It can be a very small movement. The more precise and "present" (precision demands presence) is your seeing of the punch (relationship), the more efficiently you resolve it.

If a punch is moving toward me, it is a trajectory, a line of force, actually a relatively small line (and I know where it is headed). I am the target. All I have to do is move off that line of potential force becoming a fist. If I see the punch's beginning and its line, I will just move. IF I SEE IT! Well, why wouldn't I see it? Maybe because I would be too concerned with what I should do about it to do what I should do. This is an example of when "I" would really get in the way. Yet if "I" weren't there, something would hit something and someone would get hurt.

If you rub your hands together and then hold them an inch or so apart you can feel pressure, maybe heat, maybe something else . . . but you feel something there. Repeat the earlier experiment. Hold your hand an inch from a candle flame. With short quick movements of your hand back and forth, the flame will jump. Notice again how the flame jumps when the hand is moved, not after, not as if the candle catches up to the movement, but together with the hand.

Standing in front of someone I feel pressure, maybe heat. With a partner, try being the "candle flame" and have your partner move you by his/her moving, advancing, retreating. When we are open and sensitive (and also trained towards this end), we will be moved. It is interesting that we are not moved thusly more often, but maybe we are and are not aware.

The study of Hsing I Ch'uan has as its fundamental teaching simultaneous creation and destruction. Destruction implies that within yang is yin and vice versa. In Hsing I, I destroy your "technique" as I create my own . . . not in a linear one-after-the-other fashion as in "block the punch, then punch," but simultaneously. When two people have that approach, Hsing I becomes an interesting game. The air is thick with potential and the game of discriminating between what is and what isn't also encompasses what will be. You want to realize potential—yours and your partner's—without attachment to something happening in a particular fashion. As one's skill deepens and presence becomes microscopic in detail, one "sees." Not because there is more to see, but because of a willingness to notice what is there and staying with it moment by moment.

When boxing, one must constantly open to the experience of the situation. Punching and dodging must be actively present and in appropriate response to your opponent's actions. Listening is feeling what is going on: you, your opponent, the relationship. Interpreting is knowing the potential of the relationship and meeting its demand, the demand that usually takes the shape of incoming blows, kicks, punches, etc. Meeting the demand can mean cutting potential. Through stepping, you can set distances and angles, remaking and keeping your position advantageous in relationship to your opponent. This occurrence is constantly changing in accordance with what is. Meeting the demand can be sensing occurrences prior to their taking shape. Sensing intent, you render it invalid or neutralize it either through cutting potential or hitting your opponent prior to his acting.

We can want to see and "cut" our partner's potential. It can appear obvious that if I want to move to my right, I would do it in the most efficient manner. It would be to your advantage to see what I think is most efficient, i.e., potentially how I would do it. If I want to hit you, you want to be aware of what you are offering to be hit; and then I can be led. Suddenly I realize that I am the target and there are some other, better ways for you to hit me. That information I get from you, from how you respond to me. If your head is between your left hand and my head, and your right hand is between your head and mine, the potential—the possibility of your hitting me with your right—is greater than the possibility of your hitting me with your left. This is a rough example; the potential game gets very refined. I am still open to getting hit with your left, something you might do if you saw that I was attached to your right hand. I would not be available to dodge your kick or your left if I were focused on your hands. As you adjust, I adjust, always being open to things as they are, cutting your potential. It becomes a game of whoever is "more" present. This is of course after a repertoire of techniques has been learned and internalized.

Cultivating mindfulness and a commitment to feeling, living in and coming from the body, moment by moment, are of paramount importance, and unless these are to some degree realized, one can wander lost in the forest of techniques, looking for the technique that will make everything work.

As I have said, any technique will work. Doing what has to be done to accomplish the job (say, winning the fight) is different from looking for the right technique to finish the job. When the job is done, it will surely be finished through the execution of technique, yet technique is coincidental to the art of getting the job done. We cannot not *do* technique. Its emphasis is different. We do not want to get all messed up on technique; we want to get the job done. This way of seeing things is very radical in certain circles. It is dogma-busting.

Rick Faye, my Kali instructor in Minneapolis, has an interesting view of the arts. In a newsletter, he wrote that at the origin of every "traditional" martial art was a creative, exploratory individual, a rogue—someone usually outside the tradition—who was different from his contemporaries. Unorthodox and effective, he did what worked. What was communicated in the teachings of these individuals was basically the techniques of *their* art. These techniques were handed down and a "traditional" martial art was established. Sincere exploration is not supported in "traditional" classes, but rather obedience to the "style." Yet this is precisely what the founder undoubtedly broke away from.

What I learned in my Kali period is the notion of each individual martial art working in a range particular to itself. For example, in Wing Chun, distance is short. It is very strong in what is called infighting, hand techniques. For martial arts that have long-range kicking techniques, like Tae Kwon Do or Sil Lum, infighting is not usually emphasized. Grappling arts such as Judo, Jujitsu, and Chinna employ what works at their particular range. "Grappling" in the other arts is almost ignored.

Fitting the martial art to the person rather than stuffing the person into a martial art is an appropriate approach.

I have a friend living in Los Angeles who has studied with the Jeet Kune Do crowd—Inosanto, Bustillo, etc.—for at least ten years. He has studied with the instructors of these people in various exotic arts such as Pentjak Silat and Savate as well as the standard IMB fare of Wing Chun, Muay Thai and Kali. In the past when we got together to play, something was missing from his approach. Or maybe there was too much in his approach.

There is a thread that binds all martial arts. Any technique can work—a Shotokan side kick, a Capoeira cartwheel—but what is involved in making it work—the entry, timing, distance—is encompassed in the study of relationship.

The main reason I may seem condescending toward technique-oriented instruction and practice is my experience of "losing" fights and "winning" fights and studying why I have won or lost. When I get uptight or hooked into what the other person is doing, I don't do so well. When I see "us" and am relaxed and open, I do better. Being caught in searching through my repertoire of moves for one that would work gets me in trouble. Filling my partner's empty spots with a blow should be determined by my partner. When and how is determined by him, not by me. I cannot hit him whenever I want to. If I experience "us," then we will work together towards my "opponent's" defeat.

When I was a younger student of internal martial arts, my teacher was talking about some of the people he had seen competing in a tournament. He told us about a Pa Kua player who looked good but had lost his bout. I asked him how this could be, since Pa Kua was fundamentally the same as T'ai Chi, and everyone knows that T'ai Chi Ch'uan is the ultimate, right? He said, "He was probably doing what he thought he should be doing, rather than what he should be doing."

Remember, if the martial arts are to remain living and vital, it is our responsibility to discover for ourselves what the founders discovered. We must not be satisfied with mimicking our teachers, parroting the philosophy.

When doing push hands, let sticking and yielding melt into simply four ounces of pressure. When retreating, four ounces; when advancing, four ounces. Two people, one thing, four ounces. When you are advancing and your partner reaches his edge, the place where the next thing for him to do is either step or lose his balance, you step in and add on—like pushing someone running away from you in the back to make them fall over forward. Every kid knows how to add on. When your partner retreats, pay lots of attention to his edge, his willingness to go to it. Stick to your retreating partner very lightly; in fact, you want to feel pulled by him, until

87

his retreat matures. At the point when your partner is between courses of action, or regaining his composure after too rigorous a retreat, step in and uproot him. This is "adding on."

Do not get hypnotized by movement; stay in your feet. Do not reach when it means leaving your root. Do not retreat if retreat is pulling away blindly trying to escape. Be patient!

We want to discover the mind out of which T'ai Chi Ch'uan appeared. Not mimic shapes. We are the art, not Snake Creeps Down or Brush Knee/Twist Step. Irimi Nage is not Aikido.

Opposite Push Hands

In opposite push hands the roles of initiator and yielder are reversed while each maintains the classic ward-off, rollback, press and push. For example: A, the pusher, has his hands on his partner's wrist and elbow. B, the person in the ward-off position, rather than waiting and responding to A's push, initiates by leading. The pusher responds by sticking to B's rollback. B also leads A's press all the while A is sticking and blending. A is being pulled by B leading. The feeling of being pulled can be felt on the backs of the hands rather than the front only. After the press is initiated by B, the roles are reversed. B, who is now in the position of pushing, sticks to A's rollback.

This exercise breaks up the hypnotizing choreography of push hands and forces the participants to respond to the partner's action. Eventually the "boundary" between yielding and initiating breaks down and the availability of leading everything in Tui Sho at all times is seen. This exercise demands the mindful participation of the T'ai Chi players. The words "sticking," "yielding," and "leading" become one's own experience.

An exercise for practicing adding-on is as follows: two people, one A, one B. B is in the position of push; A is in the ward-off position. Either A or B can initiate; ultimately it does not matter since whenever your partner retreats—whether or not he is leading—you stick to his action. For example, even the person in the push position can lead. If we push our partner and he yields by trying to get away or outrun the push, we can lead him by applying the right pressure at the right time. He runs; we follow. When we want them to change direction, we apply pressure at the right time and place. He runs and we follow all the way to his edge. There we add on and uproot.

Anyway, back to the exercise. A pushes B in ward-off. Let us say A initiates and both have the right foot forward. B is offering his/her left arm to the pusher. A initiates, and B, rather than leading A's push out to B's left side in a rollback, crosses his right arm under A's left. Here we have B's left forearm under A's right hand, and B's right forearm under A's left wrist. B leads A's push while separating his/her hands. B can lead A off his front leg (that is great), but for the purpose of the exercise say A gets to his front edge (or too close for comfort) and pulls away towards the rear. B sticks to this retreat with hands on his partner's torso. This is done as soon as A retreats, not before. Wait for the retreat. Stick and follow (or lead) your partner to his edge, add on and uproot.

Opportunities are always available. Push hands is a game in which we have many opportunities to defeat ourselves. The reasons for defeat or victory are not necessarily a matter of inferior or superior techniques, but of inferior or superior listening ability. Do not be confused here. When I say technique, I mean the technique's appearance, its shape separate from the internal qualities such as listening and blending, which are a continuous occurrence. True, one can say the internal qualities are also techniques. The problem arises when one confuses or replaces the internal qualities—which are the presence and participation of the player—with the planning of which physical technique the player thinks he or she should perform.

Here I will introduce the skill of "cutting time," which I hope will clarify what listening is and how its use empowers the player. We will start with an illustration. Let us propose we have an amount of time, say five seconds. In that space of five seconds, let us say there are moments or occurrences of present awareness, present energy, etc., as illustrated by dots. Between the moments of awareness are intervals of whatever else arises, say thoughts concerning judgement, planning, etc., or simply spacing out. Cutting time is adding more dots of awareness to the points of a continuum of present feeling-awareness.

In the push-hands relationship, the person who is cutting time sees more, is more aware of opportunities. It is as if his partner is moving in slow motion and thus can be easily led.

As I noted earlier, leading involves opening ourselves and offering vulnerable targets to our partner. Doing so entails an acceptance of "what is" in such a way that maintains our own advantageous position. This is one of the beautiful paradoxes of T'ai Chi Ch'uan. We are continually surrendering to the situation through offering ourselves and putting ourselves in vulnerable positions (from our partner's point of view), yet leading the partner and maintaining our own advantage.

Important Distinctions

    Leading/Pulling away

    Coming from the ground/Double-weighted

    Listening/Seeing what we want to
    or seeing filtered by contrivance

    Responding/Reacting

    Upper-body strength = Double-weighted

For instance, we can offer some resistance so our partner will oppose with force. Often his force will come from upper-body strength. The more he pushes with his strength, the more double-weighted he becomes, severing himself from a sense of root.

We have many options here: we can absorb his strength and put it on the ground through our feet; we can "leverage" him off the ground (uproot). We can disappear, make a hole for him to fall into, as if he is pushing against a wall that suddenly disappears, unsettling him to the point of his falling over his own feet; or if he realizes his "error" and pulls back in order to not pitch forward, we simply stick to (follow) his retreat and "add on" when he reaches his edge.

When our partner "goes into reaction" over what we are doing or what we represent, we can steer him to his own defeat.

If we meet another's movement with resistance, we disclose what we identify with—that which is vulnerable—and give our partner the route that leads to it. The priority in the game (two-person work) is to not resist the intention of our partner. In push hands, when my movement is met with my partner's resistance, I either uproot him or go around the resistance, giving me the opportunity to attack deeper into his territory. I know where his resistance is because I simply feel it; he prevents, through force, my approach to his body. If pushed—keep in mind these are push-hand pushes—I want to allow him to move where "he wants" without being "caught" or finding my center. This is accomplished through leading, being elusive with my center, baiting with it . . . and disappearing.

Push hands is not a fighting art; it is not a game typically suited for competition unless strict rules are applied. Unless one is very skillful at push hands, strength wins. The films of

91

push hands competitions that I have seen show that push hands quickly degenerates into something less than, but akin to, wrestling. Push hands is an arena in which we have the opportunity to study skills like listening, blending, leading, borrowing, and uprooting. We study compression and effortless power. Push hands is a rather narrowly defined game—no hitting, for example. Fighting is wide open. If we play with a friend, we don't want to break his arm; there is agreement. Not so on the street.

A warming-up, loosening-up exercise that I do every class is one Peter Ralston often had us do. His teacher, William Chen, did it too in the classes I attended. I wonder if Cheng Man-Ch'ing, William Chen's teacher, did. Stand facing your partner and choose who will push and who will receive. With one hand pushers push through their partner's shoulder, either one. The receiver simply allows himself to be pushed. When our shoulder is pushed, we accommodate it, let the force turn our hips. Pushers push straight through and do not follow their partner's shoulder around as they turn their pelvis. This is not a four-ounce yielding game. The receiver often needs a push of pounds to be effectively moved.

Receivers do not lead, but are simply moved. Pushers move the partner's relaxed meat. In this way, for the receiver it is a game of allowing oneself to be moved, *without helping or pulling away*. The receiver's arms hang and flop as his body is moved. Pushers also push the receiver's hips, specifically the crest of the ilium, the hip bone. The receiver "breaks" in the middle and sticks his butt out to accommodate the push. Receivers could accommodate a hip push by turning their waist, but that will not suffice to diffuse even a moderately deep push. These are smooth, slow, straight pushes. Pushers are helping the receivers to relax. Also, receivers do not step and do not stand double-weighted. Like the clown punching-dummy with the heavy base, the receiver, after being pushed, comes back to neutral, relaxed and in his feet.

This game can be turned up. Shoulder, hip, hip, hip, shoulder, hip, etc; either shoulder, either hip. The pushes are not abrupt and punchy, but straight and deep, one after another. It is a great game.

An adaptation is when the receiver starts participating in the push, starts leading. Remember, leading is not pulling away. The pusher feels as though he is falling into a hole. From there the receiver can start creating stuff, seizing advantages. Play around! This game can be inserted into regular choreographed push hands; it can be improvised and dropped if it gets too much. It's the beginning of formless push hands. While in I was New York attending classes, William Chen told our group that to get good at push hands we had to be good at this exercise.

When yielding to a force within the game of push hands in which there is continuous contact between partners, it is important (very) to feel the direction of the incoming force. I often call that direction a line, a line of force. When we feel the line and the "speed" of the push (the speed can be gauged as how fast the push would travel if we were to suddenly disappear), we first must yield (move) in the direction of the push. We want to blend with the force; there is no warding off, parrying, or fighting with the force. We blend and then we can move the target (what our partner is aiming for) off the line. This (a miss) can be accomplished by keeping the pusher's hands on our arm if we are doing a ward-off and moving our bodies off the line through blending—keeping our partner's attention (and hand) stuck to our arm—and leading the push astray. Often it is a combination of the two. What is appropriate is determined by the situation.

The difference between leading a force and pulling away from the force is very clear; yet the two are very close to each other. We can pull away and if our partner is led, then it worked; if we start to lead—that is to say, it is working and our partner suddenly changes his direction—we have to adjust and lead him without a struggle or we would be pulling away. The difference is clear yet subtle. If our partner is good at destroying leading or very good at leading, we have to keep our priorities straight. I have to stop pushing my partner's arm if his arm is no longer a route to his center. It is the game of "keep my center hidden." My center is my core, "where I live"; it is the body that can be caught and uprooted. Catching someone's center is finding his substantiality; uprooting him is severing him from the ground (his root) and projecting him away.

Substantial and insubstantial, filling and emptying, yin and yang are shop words in T'ai Chi Ch'uan dogma. If I were to push you, you would be met with my substantialness, my fullness; you would want to empty, turning insubstantial what I am pushing. This is yielding; you would want to attack my substance and I would want to empty it . . . and so it goes.

As I touch someone, I know his "weight." His "weight" is a collection of components. They are: what foot he has his weight on, how close to his edge he is, where his attention is, if he pulls away from or "embraces" my touch, the direction he is moving (if he is), or where he wants to (if he is not, there is always motion). What also is necessary to catch his weight (ever changing) is choosing which direction and angle (how) to uproot him (if possible). It seems like a lot, yet it is one thing, weight. I want his "weight in my hands." When touched by another, I want to feel my partner's weight and to what he is committed (his push, its speed and angle). Feel the line; feel his potential for both "creation and destruction." Feeling another's weight has as its foundation our own "body mechanics," our own weight and its components, our potential for movement, chin or attention, and edge.

Riding the wave before the meat of the punch or the push is critical to me. Before the hand comes a field, a wave of pressure that can move the dodger ahead of it. My sense of this field is what the T'ai Chi classics describe as cultivating a quality of lightness. I must be sensitive like a feather in the wind yet firmly planted in the ground—both planted, and very light and mobile. Then step where your partner is disadvantaged; if he/she follows, seduce their intention by offering tasty targets, pulling them off their feet, encouraging their clumsiness, yet blinding them to their own ineffectiveness by looking vulnerable, all the time urging them to try.

In fighting or push hands, be continually listening to your partner. When I am surprised by what my partner does it is usually because I have my own plan, am doing my own strategy. In boxing, we can start bobbing and weaving, dodging as a reflection of our partner, or bobbing and weaving out of what we think is happening. If our partner sees our delusion he can simply fill in the gaps between "what is" and what we are reacting to. He can realize what he does to elicit our reactions and continue to do so or play around. This is internal boxing.

Cultivate a sucking quality in your relationship to your partner: a touch-me, hit-me aspect. It is what they are going to do anyway, so give them something to touch, or hit, or pay attention to. Do not be attached to their touching in a particular way, and don't judge yourself or them if you are caught in your own plan. Simply come back to the present relationship. Find ways to use what your partner does to your own advantage. See what he sees. Know what he wants, and what gets him to act. Do the game (boxing, for example) in slow motion; dodge in a way that will put you in a position of advantage, a place where your weapon is close to a target and where your targets are inaccessible, or simply bait to further your partner's disadvantage. This often can be accomplished through stepping. With stepping we manipulate distance, angles, position, all at once. Where we are will determine where they are going.

"Seduction" is another way of describing leading. We always want to entice our partner with targets that are in a comfortable place for them to reach. It is obvious that instead of simply responding to our partner's actions (which takes mindfulness and skill), we are actively creating our partner's action. If they don't play along and go for the targets given (we don't want them to know we are aware of our targets), we must be available to lead whatever target they do go for. I make a clear distinction between leading and running, or pulling away. A moving target is harder to hit, but it isn't leading.

This way of being with another demands our being open to things as they are. We must feel ourselves deeply. When we feel deeply, vulnerability arises. I make a distinction between vulnerable advantageousness and vulnerable disadvantageousness. Being open and aware, we are indeed open to being hurt; we also have an awareness of how to maintain an advantage because we are not closing off what we don't want to see (feel). More information is available. We can see and feel from which direction, how fast, etc., the push or punch of our opponent is coming. Often when I appear most vulnerable to my partner I am in my best position to lead, since people who are vulnerable have fewer options (or at least that is what I want my partner to think and act on).

It is also important to distinguish between investing in loss and just losing. *Learning instead of going into denial.*

Often it has happened when working with beginners in push hands that I catch them on the back foot yet not near their edge. Suddenly they give up. They believe that I have got them when actually they have many options. They feel vulnerable, and they are. Yet vulnerability does not mean losing or going weak or that it's time to give up. It is the source of our information. We are always vulnerable. Everything can hurt us. To feel deeply demands courage; to stay awake and open under duress gives us the opportunity to effectively change our circumstances.

It is best that we ally our "opponent's" intent with our own, up to a point (they don't win); yet in actuality there is not this qualification. We do not interfere with their activity, we do not oppose their strength, we do not try to change their mind, or "talk" them into anything. We do not force our will upon them. We win through deep interaction; our "opponent" learns that it is to his advantage to be nonviolent.

In the heat of battle we, with clarity and insight, mold ourselves around our opponent's intent, attention (lack of and adding onto), and action—moving them, pulling them with our leading, and if "required," giving them the impactful feedback that violence is painful.

Freefighting is an arena in which the intensity that permeates my relationship to my "opponent" is a demand which cannot be ignored, lest I receive a blow. The clarity and calm demanded in the center of such a cyclone brings to bear the full account of my skill and also makes plain where I fall short.

I want to see what my opponent sees, to know what motivates his action and what he hopes to accomplish. What are his conditions for the attempt? What threatens him, what emboldens him is what enables me to lead him with what he wants. Seeing him see his opportunity, blinding him to my attack. Not judging any loss or gain, but surrendering, molding myself to him, on and on to his defeat. Baiting and leading his strength and attacking his weakness, not giving myself the opportunity to fight his strength out of bravado or right-eousness but being patient, not trying to force him to fit my strategy but ultimately seducing him to fit my strategy.

Freefighting is a study that calls upon all the resources at one's command—every facet of our being, our presence. The willingness or not to participate in such a game does not seem like so big a decision. Yet when turned up, when the participants' intent is to press and break the limits of their skill, the decision to participate is ever-present. All that has been assumed about such a confrontation is quickly defeated; whatever is internalized is challenged continual-ly. We find grace under pressure, and a powerful commit-ment to be open to the situation. To feel everything yet not be spun off into reaction and judgment is an empowering training of awareness. It can also be an opportunity for a superior fighter to reinforce his/her habits and assumptions while "winning" over a less experienced or simply a less skilled fighter. I have done both. One can slide by in a haze of false assumptions for years, an entire lifetime, while appar-ently "winning." Then it is time to invest in loss.

Thich Naht Han teaches that if I am told by another that I am ugly or unworthy, I am moved. I am moved by what another says to me. Mere words affect me. Actions more so.

Perhaps if you say I am ugly, I know I am not, yet I am moved that you should say so. I am hurt. Not that I am ugly but that another would try to hurt me so. We are connected, deeply; we are one being at war with itself. Is it perhaps true that one individual cannot attain enlightenment until we all (the one) do?

The Game

So, here we are, facing each other. The game is boxing. No maiming, no breaking of bones; we don't even have to hit hard. In fact, let's not for now . . . maybe later.

I see you; you see me; wait, let's go back a few "steps." I experience; you experience; I see, hear, feel something; you see, hear, feel something. We also have thoughts; let's assume that at least we are thinking about the event before us. We face each other, each with the intention of playing and winning a particular game. Fear is up; caution is up; intimidation is up. . . . Denial is up. We each see more and less than what is going on. Just facing each other. I see you seeing me; you see me seeing you. Here it is important to realize that how clearly we actually are "being with" what is happening determines what we see. I move and your eyes follow me; you adjust your position to better your ability to deal with what you think will happen next. Since the game is "boxing" let's say you think I am looking for ways of hitting you and not getting hit. I see you do this. I notice any lag, any catch-up time between my movement and your adjustment. In your adjustment I see what you want to protect, your body obviously, maybe more, maybe less. In your adjustment I see to what degree your movement reflects mine, or if you have your own agenda. I also see how you move, if you are awake, if you have the availability of changing mid-stride, quarter, eighth or tiny stride, or have the tendency to make a plan, decide to carry it out, start carrying out your plan, and in carrying it out, space out or become involved in the formulation of more plans. You see that I have read you rather clearly; you see what I have missed, what I have added on. We are both awake. You say, "Look, if you surrender now, I will buy you a beer." I say Okay.

Scenario B: The game continues.

You step within my range, I hit you, you surrender, I buy you a beer.

Scenario C: The game continues.

You step within what you feel is my range in such a way that I am offered a target. You do this very mindfully, open to accommodating an attack, open to reflecting an attack by, let's say, dodging a punch and filling the "hole" I create by throwing a punch. You are in your feet, loose, I see I am being baited; I throw a slow punch. Piece by piece, millimeter by millimeter, moment by moment, if my punch is rendered obsolete by any action on your part, I am open to change. You dodge what you think is a fast punch. You dodge; yet in your dodging you have a plan. You think my punch is dead. I bend my elbow turning my missing straight punch into a hook, also stepping to the side away from the hand you would hit me with if your plan were to work. Yet you come into your body here, dropping the notion of hitting me in your dodge. You feel the side of your head that is now my target, and you lead with it; you let my punch happen. I think, "I got you." You duck as I am punching, throwing a punch (apparent) as soon as physically possible. I feel your target and step back. I say, "Hey, you're pretty good." You say, "So are you. Thirsty?"

Upon asking people who box or spar why they do it, I am often told about the intensity, the clarity under pressure, the center-of-the-cyclone quality of mindfulness, the truthfulness of the relationship. There are no personalities to be humored. If we are not present we get hit; if we are involved in our own agenda we get hit; if we are pulling away or refuse to participate fully in the game we get hit. If in any way we are not deeply engaged in what is happening and committed to being engaged, blending with our partner, surrendering to his or her activity, we get hit. We want to surrender to their activity, allowing them to "tell us" when to attack, where to move, how fast, etc., so eventually we can hit them. The quality of mind required to accomplish this is what makes the art so satisfying.

You are doing great. But don't get hypnotized by the drama. Stay sober.

It is obvious to me why I box, and yet I have people in my life who simply think it is crazy.

Typically in the martial arts you will find quite a bit of competition, resentment, and a willingness—even a preference—to destroy that which is not like oneself. An old theme. People typically study martial arts so they may be better armed against, and a better fighter against, whatever they fear. A greater arsenal ensures our victory. People who "carry" weapons often carry them out of fear. Typically people learn the martial arts for narcissistic reasons.

The ideal Samurai carried weapons out of service to his lord. This is the ideal: to hold the power and clarity of warriorship out of service; to use our swords to cut through self-delusion, confusion, and arrogance.

A story: Padmasambhava the man, the bodhisattva who brought Buddhism to Tibet, entered a land where Shaman-

101

ism, magic, held sway. Powerful entities, spirits, a whole pantheon of dangerous forces in the arsenal of those who had the means. At night many of these forces hung out at a particular graveyard. Padmasambhava went, against the advice of the people, to that graveyard to meditate at night. Everybody knew "they" would be there and tear Padmasambhava apart. Padmasambhava arrived; he sat; they appeared. Padmasambhava touched their suffering, and through his compassion and understanding, the forces allied themselves with Padmasambhava and Buddhism. He did not convert them; I don't think he convinced them by talking them into it or presenting superior arguments. They joined him because he touched them. These forces are the Yidams, the guardians, protectors of virtue and destroyers of confusion in the Vajrayana tradition of Tibetan Buddhism.

A warrior can cut through crap and touch another's tenderness, the part that loves children, feels pain, and would rather be friends. To do so takes power. If one's actions are hollow, lacking substance, this is easily detected and resented. A warrior walks his talk. We have to be in touch with that part of us that loves children, feels pain, and would rather be friends. It is not to our advantage to go around looking for enemies to defeat.

With the power of surrender I need not kill or even hurt. Their flame will die all by itself. I need not interfere.

Afterword

I have a friend who has mentioned that he would not mind being in the Middle East preparing for war. A soldier. Something about an arena in which to study, train, manifest the ability to kill, cleanly. A clean kill. Without anger, or bitterness, but in service. You know, like a samurai, to die in the service of one's lord, to live with the immediacy of death, the Bushido code.

I have two other friends, one a falconer, one an ex-T'ai Chi Ch'uan instructor. I have spoken to both about the relativity of Lao Tzu's Taoism. For every yes, a no; every good, a bad; every red, a blue; to become attached to something is foolish because it is going to go away. I am often attached to this idea. For many years the three of us have had good dreams, but we can't seem to make any of them happen. It is hard to know how to act, what to do, to realize one's work in the world when making the necessary choices and carrying them out are seen as uncool from that Taoist way. Nonattachment is seen as more appropriate to one's spiritual growth. This notion is certainly true in martial arts. Attachment to events happening a particular way, clinging to past events through judging or anticipating, strategizing, gets one into big trouble. It hurts to get hit, even when defending a good cause. Coming back into one's body after receiving a painful blow demands a sharp sword, cutting away everything but the present.

Is it morally right to correct the behavior of someone who is uncaring and arrogant concerning the rights of others? Or should we say to ourselves, "That is what is happening," and "surrender," not doing anything. Whether it is someone throwing his Snickers wrapper on the hiking trail or attacking another person, we live in a time and place (in the United States) where the right to be who we are has been perverted into the right to pollute and to raise our children the way we want. On a bus in Minneapolis, I watched a woman verbally abuse her son in a very shaming and righteous manner. I was moved to ask her to lighten up so her angry young son wouldn't grow into an angry young man. I didn't speak out of fear of retaliation. She would not have heard it, and I am sure the line, "Don't tell me how to raise my kids" would have come up. We have the "right" to be individuals against others. "I" am more important than "you." If you don't like my litter, *you* pick it up. Would it be appropriate for me to pick up someone's litter and put it in his pocket? I don't know if it would work. They might swing at me and I would have to take them down. That would satisfy my anger, but it would not teach them anything except not to litter where others can see.

Even now there is anger in me. Sitting here in the woods I hear noises in back of me. The sound of humans. Now I am the type of person who, if given the choice, would rather not be seen in the woods. I fantasize these people approaching me where I sit. Immediately I see options of defense, including feeling myself standing in back and to the left of me while I sit. I feel the ground, checking out compression, ready to go. Then suddenly I am in my body, and I wish them peace, that they come to me with no violence in them. That is how I would rather be, to have compassion as the ground upon which I make my decisions.

We want to feel everything, to be in the world with enthusiasm and interest. In the Samurai tradition the cherry blossom represented the beauty, the glory of life . . . and then death, and the transitory nature of our existence. We want to adopt a "cherry blossom" attitude towards life. Appreciation is strong. Don Juan spoke often to Carlos about the immediacy of life that is available when one lives with the awareness of death. We do not have time to spend in confusion.

Yesterday I walked along Briones Crest. Looking east towards the Central Valley I saw a layer, an inversion cloud of pollution so thick I could not see the base of Mt. Diablo. The difference between the brownish murk separated by a clean line to the bright blue was striking. I was with a friend who remarked that if an Aborigine to this land could have beheld such a sight he would have seen it as a blight against the land, a calamity, something evil to be warded off. What can a martial artist do? Become active in politics, campaigning, lobbying, writing Congresspeople? The government seems to protect the right of big business to pollute and restricts research in soft technology and alternatives to oil. Earth First!? Approach the battlefield with a wrench, protecting trees by sleeping in them?

There seems to be a last great battle before us, so I wonder at the apathy and helplessness that marks the times. What to do? As things worsen I think that in a few years we will have no choice but to choose a side. Feel it! Feel it!